CHECK OUT THIS IMAGE! IT LOOKS LIKE THESE PATHS WARP AND WEAVE ACROSS THE PAGE, BUT IN FACT THE IMAGE CONSISTS OF LOTS OF L SHAPES ARRANGED IN PERFECT DIAGONALS. THE REST IS CREATED BY YOUR BRAIN.

P9-BYM-756

NATIONAL
GEOGRAPHIC
KiDS

BRAIN GAMES

COLOSSAL BOOK OF CRANIUM CRUSHERS

STEPHANIE WARREN DRIMMER
AND DR. GARETH MOORE

NATIONAL GEOGRAPHIC
WASHINGTON, D.C.

CONTENTS

CHAPTER ONE
GREETINGS, GENIUS

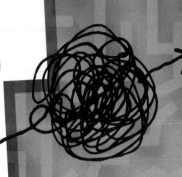

RIGHT NOW, YOUR HANDS ARE GRIPPING THIS BOOK. The pages feel smooth beneath your fingers. Your eyes are moving back and forth as you read. In the background, you might hear people talking or smell dinner cooking. And it's all made possible by your brain.

Your brain is a small organ, roughly the size of your two clenched fists. But it is mighty. Your brain takes in information from your eyes, ears, nose, and mouth and uses it to make sense of the world around you. At the same time, it controls all your thoughts, your feelings, your dreams, and your emotions. How does a little lump of tissue do all that?

That's exactly what people have been wondering for thousands of years. Brain science has come a long way from the time of ancient Egypt, when the organs of the dead were carefully preserved during the mummification process—all except for the brain. Thought to be useless, it was tossed out with the trash! Modern brain scientists, or neuroscientists, have uncovered all kinds of astounding secrets about the brain: It's controlled by electricity that zaps through your nerves; its largest portion—30 percent—is devoted to vision; and it can even rewire itself as you learn.

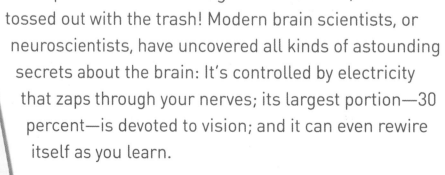

Everything we know about the brain has come from observing and doing experiments. The first scientists to dissect human bodies learned what the brain looked like. Later, experts observed the behavior of people who had suffered brain injuries to work out how the brain functioned. Today, neuroscientists use high-tech devices and techniques to explore the brain's inner workings.

This book will help you discover a little bit about how your own brain works. Use your brainpower to solve puzzles, and learn what's going on between your ears as you do it. It's a cranial challenge, but don't worry. You have the world's most powerful thinking machine to help you out: your brain!

SO PUT ON YOUR THINKING CAP, AND LET THE BRAIN GAMES BEGIN! →

BRAIN SCIENCE IS BORN

PEOPLE HAVE BEEN CURIOUS ABOUT THE BRAIN SINCE ANCIENT TIMES.

Nearly 4,000 years ago, doctors in ancient Egypt wrote a text on papyrus that described 27 different types of head injuries and how to treat them. But they mistakenly believed thoughts came from the heart, not the head. Fast-forward to 350 B.C., and the brain still wasn't getting credit: Famous thinker Aristotle thought it was nothing more than an air conditioner that cooled down the heart!

GETTING A CLOSER LOOK

Why the case of mistaken identity? Ancient people had no way to investigate the body's inner workings. They believed people would need their bodies in the afterlife, and so dissecting a dead body to see how it worked was a really bad idea. Most cultures had laws that kept people from dissecting and experimenting on dead bodies. As a result, they had no way to figure out how parts of the body—including the brain—worked.

One exception was ancient Egypt, where people dissected bodies as part of the mummy-making process. Around 300 B.C., two Greek doctors named Herophilus and Erasistratus got around the rules of their country by moving to Alexandria, a Greek-controlled city in Egypt. There, they started performing dissections of their own. Their discoveries were revolutionary. Erasistratus provided one of history's first in-depth descriptions of the brain. And Herophilus discovered that the network of nerves that stretched throughout the body connected back to the brain. He realized it had to be the brain, not the heart, that was in charge of thinking.

HEROPHILUS AND ERASISTRATUS

THOMAS WILLIS

GLADIATORS

BRAINS UNDER COVER

A few centuries later, around the second century A.D., a young Greek physician named Galen of Pergamum, became the chief doctor at a school for gladiators. By observing fighters who had suffered severe brain injuries, he was able to figure out that the brain not only controls our thoughts, but also our emotions and memories.

After Galen, brain science didn't make much progress for almost 1,400 years. Then, in the 1500s, a Flemish physician named Andreas Vesalius got permission to look inside human bodies for the first time since ancient Egypt. He published drawings of the body's insides that were so detailed and accurate that medical students still use them today. About a century later, an English doctor named Thomas Willis wrote the world's first textbook devoted to the brain.

Finally, brain science was getting somewhere. But it would take until the 1800s for modern neuroscience to really take off.

LEONARDO DA VINCI'S DRAWINGS

15TH-CENTURY ARTIST **LEONARDO DA VINCI** WAS FAMOUS FOR HIS INCREDIBLY LIFELIKE DRAWINGS AND PAINTINGS OF PEOPLE. AN EXPERT IN ANATOMY, HE LEARNED HOW THE HUMAN BODY WAS PUT TOGETHER BY **DISSECTING BODIES—MORE THAN 30** IN HIS LIFETIME.

FAMOUS BRAINS

STARTING IN THE 1800s, SCIENTISTS DID MORE THAN JUST DISSECTIONS: THEY BEGAN STUDYING PEOPLE WITH BRAIN INJURIES AND DOING EXPERIMENTS TO LEARN HOW THE BRAIN WORKED. THEIR DISCOVERIES FORMED THE FOUNDATION OF EVERYTHING WE KNOW ABOUT THE BRAIN TODAY.

AN ACCIDENTAL DISCOVERY

In 1848, a railway worker named Phineas Gage suffered a terrible accident: Dynamite underneath a metal rod he was driving into the ground exploded, sending the iron bar flying right through Gage's head. Incredibly, Gage survived. But his brain injury caused his personality to change. Gage had been a calm man, but after the accident he became angry. He suddenly had a hard time making decisions, and he often became confused. Scientists realized that the front part of Gage's brain, where the rod had passed through, must have something to do with how people act. It was the first evidence that this part of the brain, called the frontal cortex, controls personality and behavior.

PHINEAS GAGE

WORDS ON THE BRAIN

In 1861, an unusual patient walked into the office of French doctor Paul Broca. The man could only say one word, "tan." (Otherwise, he had relatively normal brain function and wanted to communicate!) Broca wondered if his speech problems came from a problem in his brain. The patient's brain was examined, and Broca's theory was proven right: The man had damage to a region of the left side of his brain. Broca had discovered the part of the brain that controls speech. Then, in 1874, a German doctor named Carl Wernicke was working with patients who had another type of speech problem—they could talk, but their words didn't make sense. Wernicke discovered that each of these patients had damage to a different area of the brain that controls how people understand and create language. Today, these two parts of the brain are named Broca's area and Wernicke's area, after the scientists who discovered them.

tan

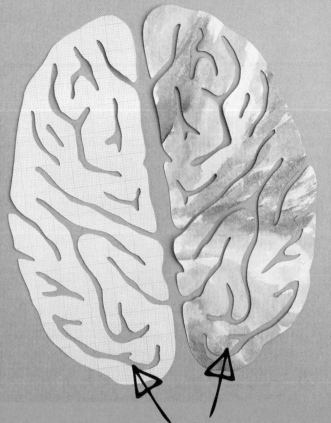

SWAPPED SIDES

Researchers began to map which parts of the brain perform which functions near the end of the 1800s, when two German doctors named Eduard Hitzig and Gustav Fritsch did experiments with electricity. They learned that zapping different areas of the brain made different parts of the body twitch. As they worked, they realized that each side of the brain controls the opposite side of the body—so that when they touched the right side of the brain with electricity, muscles on the left side of the body would react and vice versa. They had discovered something important: The right side of the brain controls the left side of the body, and the left side of the brain controls the right side of the body.

MEMORY MAKER

During the 1950s, a doctor named Wilder Penfield was trying to help patients who suffered from seizures. To figure out which brain area was misfiring to cause a seizure, he would touch an electrified wire to different parts of his patients' brains while they were awake. When Penfield touched the wire to a region called the temporal lobe, his patients would suddenly recall memories from the past, such as the color of their childhood bedroom or the sound of their dog barking. More experiments in different parts of the brain led Penfield to create the first detailed brain map.

ZAPPING THE BRAIN WITH ELECTRICITY DOESN'T HURT THE PATIENT, BECAUSE THE BRAIN HAS NO PAIN SENSORS.

IT'S ELECTRIC

Because they had discovered they could use electricity to stimulate the brain, scientists wondered: Did the brain use electricity to send its signals from one part to another? In 1924, a German scientist named Hans Berger attached electrical wires to the head using stickers, then used a machine to record the electrical energy different parts of the brain were giving off. He experimented on his 15-year-old son, Klaus, and discovered that Klaus' brain showed different types of electrical activity when he was doing different tasks, like solving math problems or imagining pictures. Berger's machine, the electroencephalograph, or EEG, was the first machine that could measure the activity of a living, working brain.

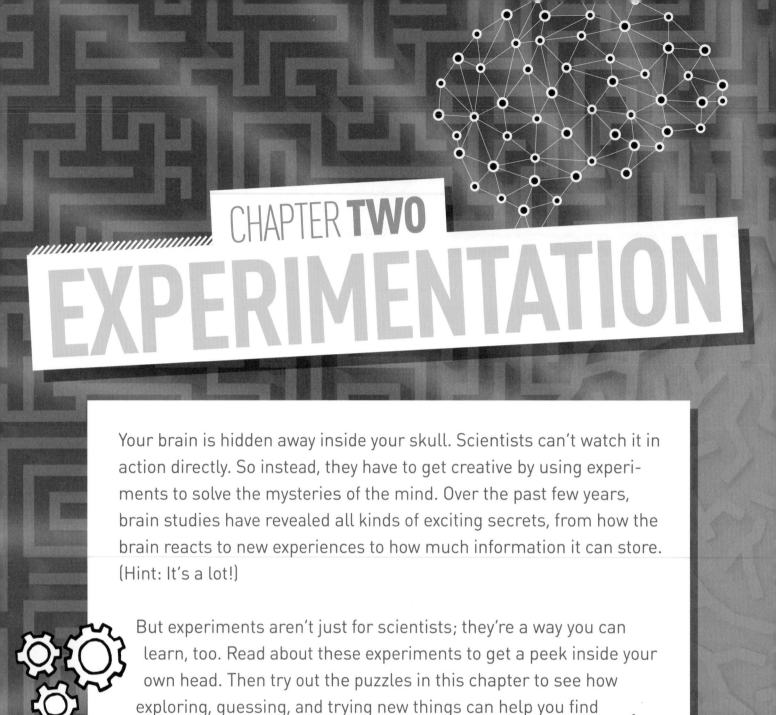

CHAPTER **TWO**
EXPERIMENTATION

Your brain is hidden away inside your skull. Scientists can't watch it in action directly. So instead, they have to get creative by using experiments to solve the mysteries of the mind. Over the past few years, brain studies have revealed all kinds of exciting secrets, from how the brain reacts to new experiences to how much information it can store. (Hint: It's a lot!)

But experiments aren't just for scientists; they're a way you can learn, too. Read about these experiments to get a peek inside your own head. Then try out the puzzles in this chapter to see how exploring, guessing, and trying new things can help you find answers in unexpected ways.

IDEA

CIRCLE **MAZE**

ANSWER PAGE 144

TRY TO FIND A PATH FROM THE ENTRANCE AT THE TOP OF THE MAZE
ALL THE WAY DOWN TO THE EXIT AT THE BOTTOM OF THE MAZE. At
first, you won't know which is the correct path. (A quick scan
of the puzzle might give you a hunch.) The only way to discover the
solution is to experiment with different paths to see where they lead.

START

FINISH

learn

TESTING THE BRAIN

READY TO BE SURPRISED BY THE POWER OF YOUR BRAIN? READ ON ABOUT SOME OF THE MOST ASTOUNDING RECENT DISCOVERIES MADE BY BRAIN SCIENTISTS.

BLINDNESS IN THE BRAIN

One-third of the brain is devoted to vision, used to process signals that come in from your eyes. But what happens to that huge portion of the brain in people who can't see? In 2018, a group of researchers compared the brains of a group of blind people with the brains of sighted people. They had both groups listen to different recordings of human speech. As the people listened to the clips, the scientists recorded the electric activity within their brains.

While the sighted people listened to the clips, an area of the brain called the auditory cortex, which processes sound, lit up with activity. The blind people showed activity in the auditory cortex, too—but they also had activity in another area: the visual cortex, which usually processes signals from the eyes. With no visual signals coming in, the brain had repurposed itself, using the visual cortex to process sound instead of sight. The experiment shows that the brain has an incredible ability to adapt and change that we are just beginning to understand.

BIT BY BIT

The human brain runs on a very small amount of energy—about 20 watts of power, barely enough to power a lightbulb. Yet, according to research from 2016, it may be capable of holding 10 times more information than scientists once thought—about the same as the entire internet!

A computer stores information using a system of two types of "bits": 1s and 0s. But a brain does far more with far less power—about 50 million times less. How? The scientists used high-powered microscopes to peer up close at synapses, the connecting points between brain cells. To their surprise, they found that synapses come in many different sizes: 26, in fact. That gives the human brain 24 more "bits" than a computer uses to store information, giving it the capacity to store as much information as the whole World Wide Web.

The study reveals that the brain is even more powerful than we realized. And someday, this discovery could lead to computers that work on a system inspired by the brain to give them much more computing ability while using far less energy.

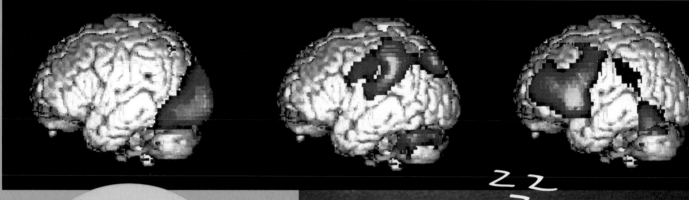

EVERY TIME WE USE OUR BRAINS— LIKE WHEN WE'RE SOLVING PUZZLES!— THEY CHANGE!

SLEEP SECRETS

As we think, our brain activity creates a buildup of substances in our brain cells: the waste products created by all that thinking. These leftovers are swept away with our cerebrospinal fluid, colorless liquid found in the brain and spinal column. In a 2013 study, scientists found that this "trash removal" process happens when we are asleep. After a period of sleep, the amount of brain waste was at its lowest. Just before sleep, the level was at its highest.

This research shows that lack of sleep doesn't just make you grumpy: It could create buildup of brain garbage that, over time, could clog your mental machine and even lead to brain diseases like Alzheimer's. So make sure to get your shut-eye!

RECTANGULAR MAZE ANSWER PAGE 144

AS YOU WIND THROUGH THIS MAZE, LEAVE MENTAL BREADCRUMBS. At which point do you shift from making a random guess—which is totally OK!—to an educated one based on the ground you've already covered? For example, you might realize there's no point in turning back because your experiments with those options "back there" have already led you to dead ends. Use the results of your experiments to reach the finish line!

START

FINISH

[BEHIND THE BRAIN]

Experimentation is one of the brain's favorite ways to learn. When you try something that works, your brain reinforces that behavior. If your experiment is unsuccessful, your brain discourages you from trying it again. This is how you learn so quickly from your trial and error. Whether you're a baby learning to walk or a kid experimenting with paths in a maze, you're experimenting in ways that are incredibly natural for your brain.

WoW!

BRIDGE MAZE ANSWER PAGE 144

YOU'RE A BIT OF A MAZE EXPERT NOW, SO IT'S TIME FOR A TRICKIER EXPERIMENT: You'll need to search high and low for the right path through this bridge maze. Sometimes you'll pass under a bridge; at other times, you'll cross over one. (And, no, you can't "jump" onto a bridge for a shortcut!) The bridges create fewer dead ends and more routes for you to experiment with. We've already gone over one bridge and under another to get you started.

START

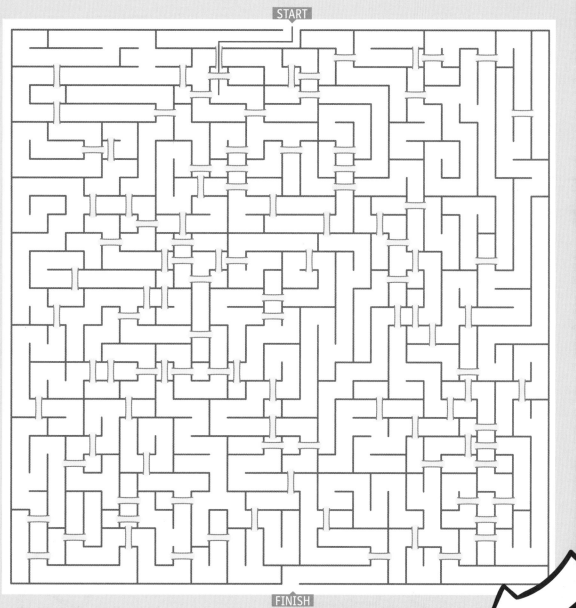

FINISH

JIGSAW CUTTING

ANSWERS PAGE 144

USING FOUR DIFFERENT COLORED PENCILS, shade in the boxes in the shapes below to divide each of the two pictures into four separate shapes. Each of the shapes within a picture must be identical, although some of them may be rotated.

HINT: Count the total number of squares in each picture, then divide by four. This will tell you how many squares each shape needs to have!

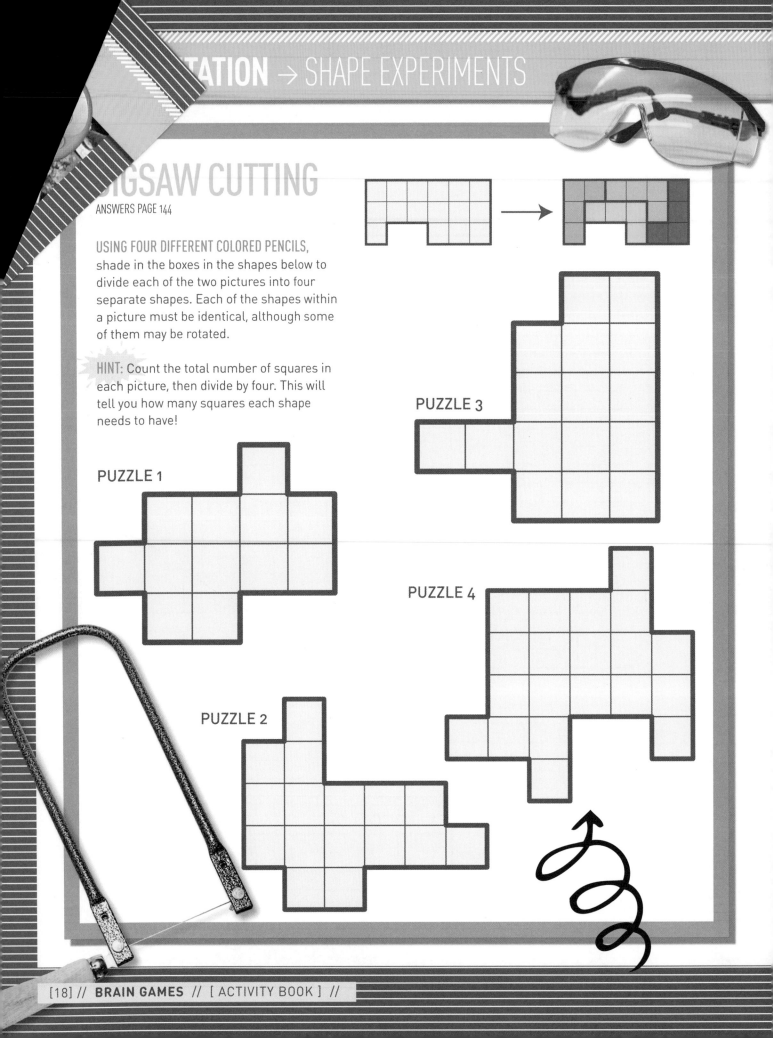

PUZZLE 1

PUZZLE 3

PUZZLE 4

PUZZLE 2

JIGSAW FIT

ANSWERS PAGE 144

EACH COLORED SHAPE ON THIS GRID NEEDS TO CONTAIN ONE CIRCLE AND ONE SQUARE. Here's the hard part: You must place the circle and square in each shape so that they do not overlap or touch a matching shape, even diagonally, anywhere on the grid. (For example, a circle can't be next to another circle.)

PUZZLE 2

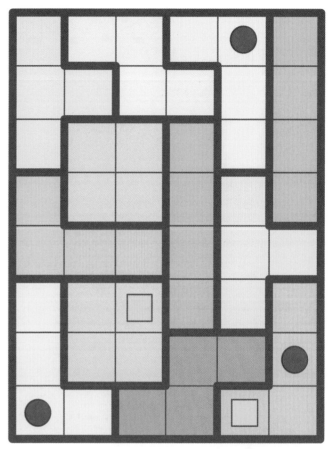

PUZZLE 1

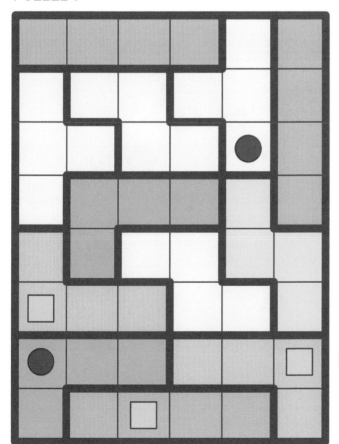

SHAPE LINK

ANSWERS PAGES 144 AND 145

THE TWO PUZZLE GRIDS BELOW CONTAIN PAIRS OF DIFFERENT SHAPES. Can you find a way to draw separate paths to connect each pair of identical shapes? Paths can travel only horizontally and vertically, and no more than one path can enter any square. This means that paths cannot cross or touch at any point.

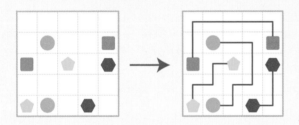

PUZZLE 1

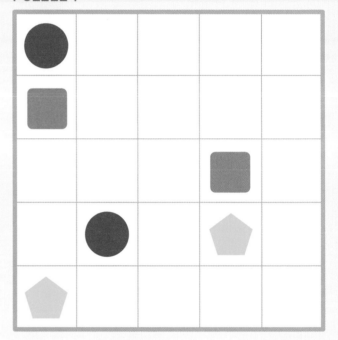

PUZZLE 2

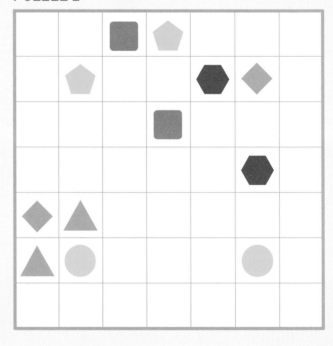

PATHFINDER

ANSWERS PAGE 145

DRAW A PATH THAT CONNECTS THE TWO SHADED DOTS, using only horizontal and vertical lines. You can use each dot only once, so the path can't cross over or touch itself. But that's not all! The numbers on the left and the top of the grid are instructions, telling you how many dots your path must cross in each row or column. For instance, if the number on the left is 3, your path should cross three dots in that row. If the number on top is 2, then your path must cross two dots in that column. Your line must cross through each row and column at least once.

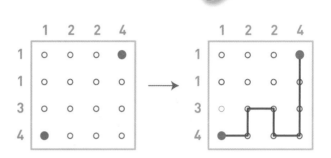

PUZZLE 1

	3	3	2	1
2	○	○	○	●
3	●	○	○	○
2	○	○	○	○
2	○	○	○	○

PUZZLE 2

	3	3	1	3	3
2	●	○	○	○	○
2	○	○	○	○	○
5	○	○	○	○	○
2	○	○	○	●	○
2	○	○	○	○	○

SIMPLE LOOP

ANSWER PAGE 145

DRAW A LOOP THAT VISITS EVERY EMPTY SQUARE ONCE, using only horizontal and vertical lines. The loop cannot cross over or touch itself at any point. Some of the squares are joined already.

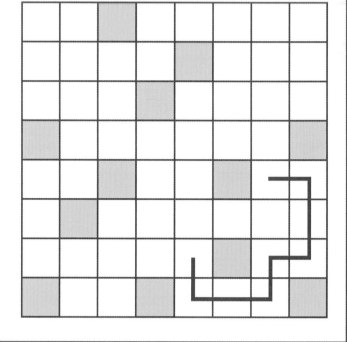

FENCES

ANSWER PAGE 145

USING ONLY HORIZONTAL AND VERTICAL LINES, CONNECT ALL OF THE DOTS TOGETHER INTO A SINGLE LOOP. The loop can visit each dot only once. This means that the loop cannot cross or touch itself at any point.

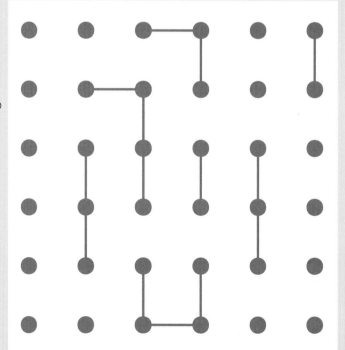

SLITHERLINK ANSWERS PAGE 145

USE THE NUMBER CLUES IN THE PUZZLE TO HELP YOU DRAW ONE LOOP WITHIN EACH GRID. Picture each number inside a box, surrounded by four sides. The number tells you how many of those four sides the loop must pass through. For example, if the number is a 3, then your loop passes through three of the four sides surrounding that number. You can use only horizontal and vertical lines. Your loop won't go through every dot, but it can visit each dot only once. **This means that the loop cannot cross or touch itself at any point.**

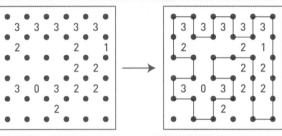

PUZZLE 1

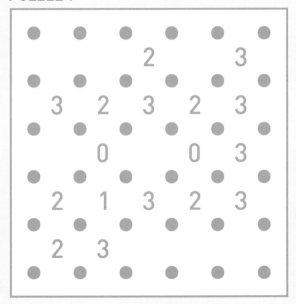

PUZZLE 2

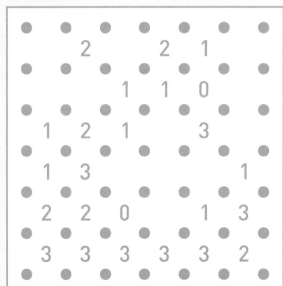

DIVIDED INTO AREAS

ANSWERS PAGE 145

CAN YOU DRAW JUST THREE STRAIGHT LINES IN THE FIRST PICTURE SO THAT YOU END UP WITH FOUR SEPARATE AREAS? Think of each area as a farm field. Each field must contain one pig, one cow, and one sheep.

For the second puzzle, draw just three straight lines to divide the sky into five separate areas. Each area must contain one cloud, one airplane, and one alien aircraft.

Here's a solved example, to show you how it works.

PUZZLE 1

PUZZLE 2

[BEHIND THE BRAIN]

When you solve puzzles like these, your brain uses a mix of experimentation and reasoning. Initially, you don't know where to start, so you dive in with some guesses. But then, you start to see that a line placed in a particular position will mean that you can't solve the puzzle, so you apply that lesson as you go. Or you might realize that there always has to be a line between identical pictures, and so you use that knowledge every time you see two of the same picture close together. This combination of reasoning and experimentation slowly moves you toward the correct solution.

MEADOWS ANSWERS PAGE 146

USE THE EXISTING LINES TO DIVIDE THE GRID INTO SMALLER FIELDS THAT EACH CONTAIN
ONE FARM ANIMAL. Every field must be square, and no grid boxes should be left over.

HERE'S AN
EXAMPLE:

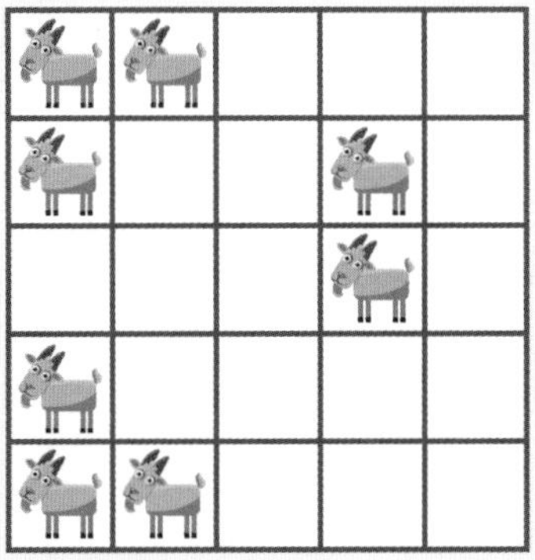

PUZZLE 1

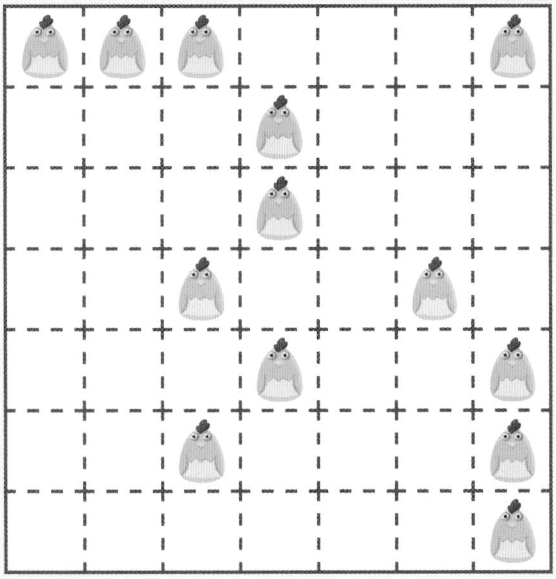

PUZZLE 2

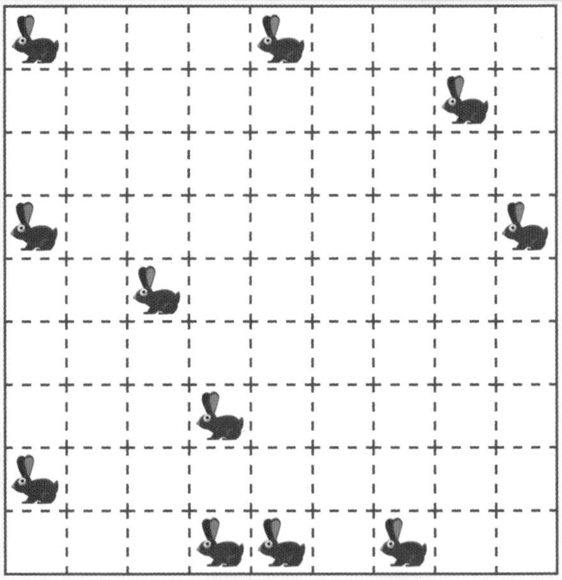

RECTANGLES ANSWERS PAGE 146

LIKE THE PREVIOUS PUZZLE, USE THE EXISTING LINES TO DIVIDE THE GRID INTO SMALLER FIELDS. This time, however, the fields can be either squares or rectangles. Each number tells you how many grid boxes should be within a field. For instance, if you see the number 9, then its field must have nine grid boxes (in a 1x9, 9x1, or 3x3 shape).

Every grid square must be in one field. To get started, look for grid squares that can only be in one field, then draw the field that reaches over to that grid square. For example, in the first puzzle, the bottom-left square must connect to the 7 above it.

PUZZLE 1

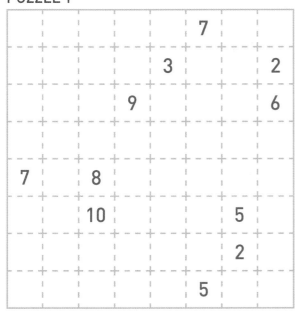

PUZZLE 2

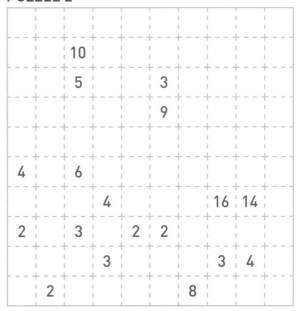

DOMINO ASSEMBLY

ANSWER PAGE 146

EACH DOMINO TILE IS DIVIDED IN HALF. Each half is either blank or has dots on it, like you would find on a die. In the game of dominoes, whenever one half of a domino touches half of another domino, those halves must match. For example, if one tile half has two dots, the touching tile half must also have two dots. If one half is blank, the other half must be blank, too. In the chain of dominoes to the right, some of the tiles have been removed. Fill in the empty spots by selecting the correct tile from below. You can rotate the loose tiles before placing them into the chain. Not all of the loose tiles will be used.

[BEHIND THE BRAIN]

Dominoes represent numbers in a visual way, with dots. Did you notice how, when solving the puzzle, you probably were matching the number of dots on the dominoes rather than the pattern of dots? Did you find yourself thinking, "I need a 6 here"? This reveals something interesting about how our brains work. When we consciously think about an image, we will often put it into words by describing it to ourselves. This shows that language is fundamental to being able to reason and think about things on a more advanced level.

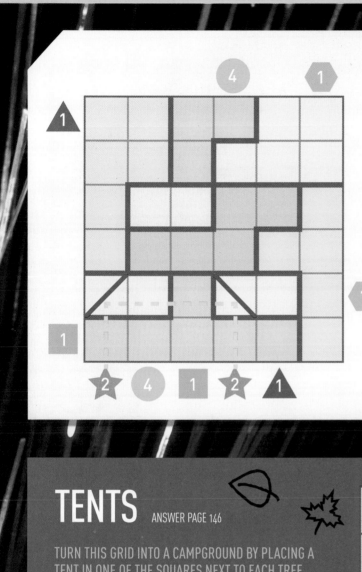

LASERS ANSWER PAGE 146

WHEN A MIRROR REFLECTS A LASER BEAM, the beam changes direction 90 degrees—a right angle. In this puzzle, you must strategically add mirrors to the grid so that you can fire a laser beam straight into the grid from one shape and have it bounce in the right direction to reach its matching shape (for example, from one triangle to another). The number inside each shape tells you how many mirrors the laser beam needs to bounce off to reach its target. You will place one mirror inside each of the bold-outlined shapes in the grid.

To get you started, some mirrors are drawn in already, along with a laser beam between the two stars to show you how it bounces.

TENTS ANSWER PAGE 146

TURN THIS GRID INTO A CAMPGROUND BY PLACING A TENT IN ONE OF THE SQUARES NEXT TO EACH TREE. The tent can be in the square above, below, or to the right or left of the tree, but not diagonal to it. To give campers privacy, tent squares cannot be next to one another, not even diagonally. When you're done, there should be one tent for every tree. Some tents are already placed on the grid.

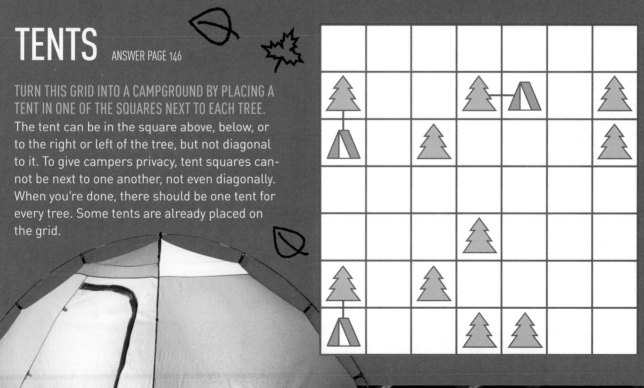

WARP MAZE

ANSWER PAGE 146

JUST LIKE *STAR TREK*, this maze uses teleporters, which magically zap you to a different location. Each of the shapes in the maze represents a teleporter. Every time your path reaches one of the teleporters, you have two choices: You can ignore the teleporter and continue on your current path, or you can enter the teleporter and warp to any other teleporter with a matching shape. Then you can carry on from that other teleporter. For example, if you reached a star square, you could either ignore the star and continue on your current path, or you could jump from there to any of the other star teleporters in the puzzle and carry on from there.

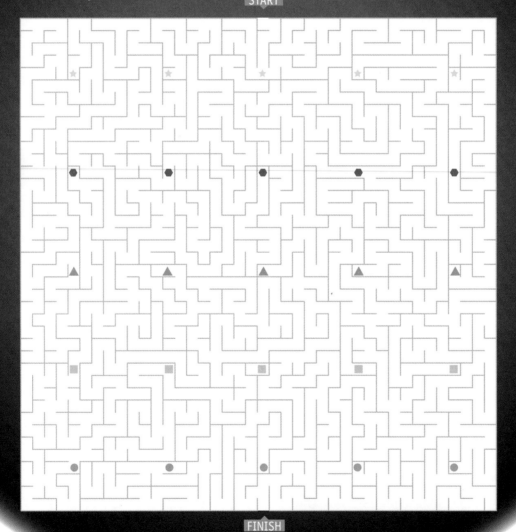

START

FINISH

MULTILEVEL MAZE

ANSWERS PAGES 146 AND 147

THINK OF THE NUMBERS IN THIS MAZE AS ELEVATORS THAT CONNECT TWO FLOORS. To make it all the way from entrance to exit on the first floor, you might have to shift to the second floor for some forward progress along the way.

Just like in the Warp Maze, you have two choices when you come to a number: You can ignore it and continue on your current path, or you can take the elevator and continue your path at the same number on the other floor.

FLOOR 1

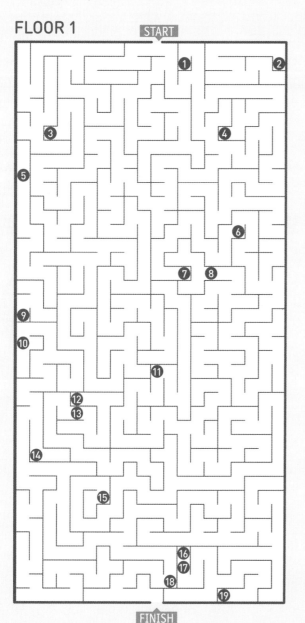

FLOOR 2

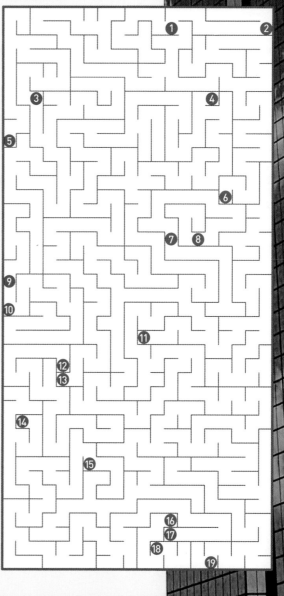

CIRCLE LINK ANSWER PAGE 147

Connect the circles into pairs by drawing horizontal and vertical lines between them. Each pair must contain one blue circle and one yellow circle. Lines can't cross each other, and they also can't cross over another circle. Every circle must be part of exactly **one** pair.

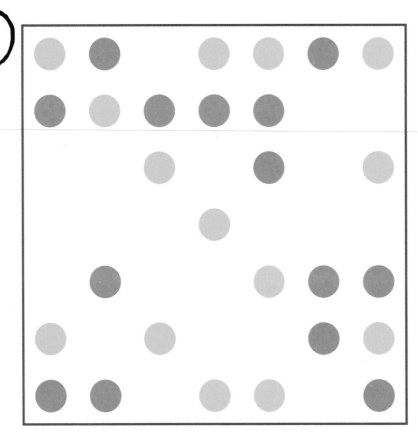

TIME STARTED

☐☐ : ☐☐

TIME ENDED

☐☐ : ☐☐

TOTAL TIME

☐☐ : ☐☐

NUMBER DARTS

ANSWER PAGE 147

The three numbers below the dartboard are your bull's-eyes, the target totals you are aiming for. Add together one number from the outer ring, one from the middle ring, and one from the inner ring so that their sum equals the first total below. Repeat the process so that your sums match the second, then the third total. You can reuse numbers for different totals.

For example, you could form a total of 15 by adding 2 from the inner ring, 4 from the middle ring, and 9 from the outer ring.

Ready, set, add!

Totals: 20 36 39

TIME STARTED   TIME ENDED   TOTAL TIME

CHAPTER THREE
LEARNING

Learning can seem like a drag. Memorizing the state capitals or the order of elements on the periodic table can be boring. But the truth is that we learn even when we're not studying for a test. Learning takes place all the time without us even realizing it: when we're discovering how to play a new game, finding our way down a new hiking trail, or remembering the words to our new favorite song.

As neuroscientists study the brain, they've discovered that the process of learning actually changes and reshapes the brain. The more knowledge you gather, the stronger your noggin. Try it out for yourself with the learning puzzles in this chapter!

→

MONUMENT **MATCHING**

ANSWERS PAGE 147

EACH OF THE IMAGES ON THIS PAGE REPRESENTS A FAMOUS LANDMARK from one of the eight countries listed below. Draw lines to join each landmark to the name of the country where it is found. There is one picture per country.

If you aren't sure of some of the answers, start by drawing the lines you do know, then see if you can guess the remaining connections.

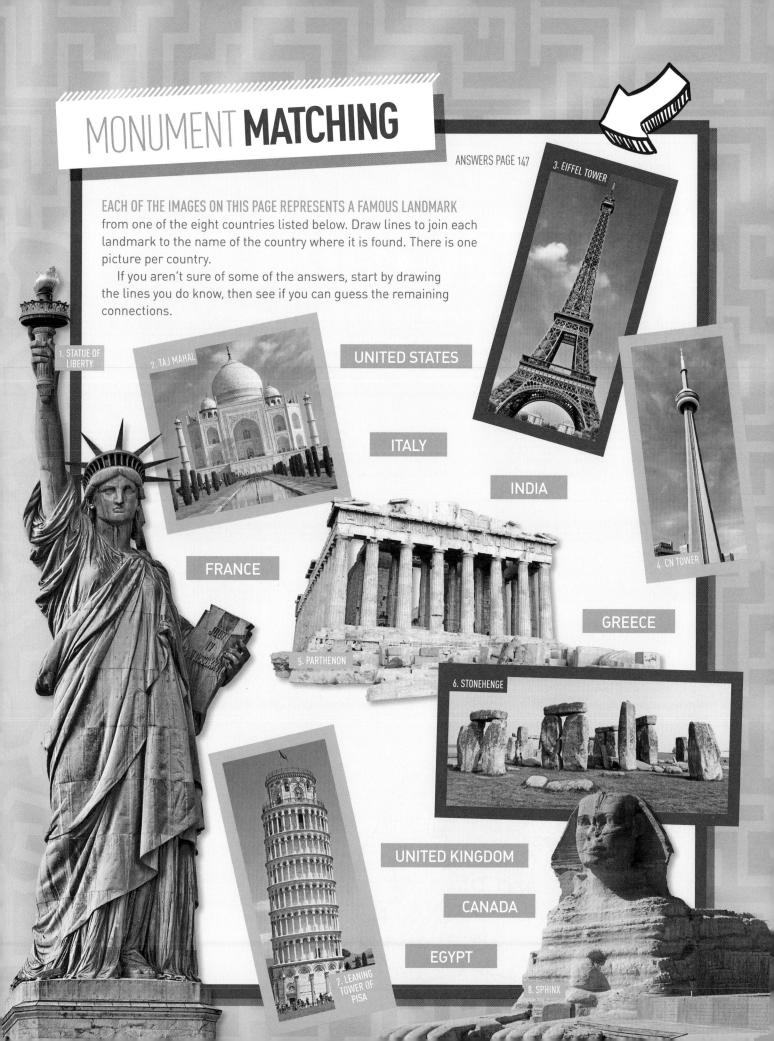

3. EIFFEL TOWER

1. STATUE OF LIBERTY

2. TAJ MAHAL

UNITED STATES

ITALY

INDIA

4. CN TOWER

FRANCE

GREECE

5. PARTHENON

6. STONEHENGE

UNITED KINGDOM

CANADA

EGYPT

7. LEANING TOWER OF PISA

8. SPHINX

MASTER YOUR MIND

WHAT IF LESSONS WERE TAUGHT IN THE WAY OUR BRAINS LEARN, SO THAT MASTERING NEW INFORMATION WAS A SNAP? WITH THE DISCOVERIES FROM THESE EXPERIMENTS, BRAIN SCIENTISTS MIGHT SOMEDAY DO JUST THAT.

HOW YOU LEARN

What's going on inside your brain when you learn something new? That's what scientists set out to discover in 2015, when they scanned the brains of 16 people while showing them a series of diagrams. These diagrams described how common objects, such as a bathroom scale and a fire extinguisher, work.

The researchers found that as the participants learned, their brain activity went through three different stages. At first, they used the visual areas of the brain to reason through the diagram. Then they imagined how the components would work together in motion. Then they used the part of the brain responsible for movement to picture how they would interact with the device. The scientists think that, eventually, research like this could help teachers present new information in a way that matches how the brain learns.

PRACTICE MAKES PERFECT

Flipping through note cards to study for a test or doing scales on a piano over and over is boring. But it's a great way to learn. That's because repetition of a task actually changes the brain.

Your brain is made of billions of nerve cells, called neurons, that "talk" to each other by sending signals from one to the next to the next. When you repeat a task over and over, the path of connections between the neurons becomes stronger. As these connections strengthen, it takes less effort for your brain to do the task. In 2013, researchers looked at 38 past studies that had analyzed the brain while a person learned a new task. They found that, at first, people used areas of the brain involved in paying close attention. But as they learned, those areas became less active. Eventually, repetition of a task allows the brain to work on autopilot, so the person can daydream—or think about nothing at all—while playing a piece of music or hitting a baseball.

SKILL SHARE

It can take years to learn a new language or master an instrument. Wouldn't it be nice if, instead, you could simply download that knowledge instantly into your brain? It sounds like science fiction, but one day, it may be possible.

In 2018, scientists taught snails to withdraw into their shells when researchers tapped on them by using small zaps of electricity. Once the snails had been trained, they would react by retreating into their shells for about 50 seconds. Then the scientists took a sample of genetic material from these snails and transferred it to snails that hadn't had the training. When their shells were tapped, these new snails reacted much like the trained snails, withdrawing into their shells for about 40 seconds. A "control group" of untrained, unaltered snails spent just a second or so inside their shells when tapped.

This experiment shows that memories—which some scientists believe are stored in genetic material—can be transferred from one snail to another. We're a long way from doing the same thing in humans, but in the future, it just might be possible.

CHANGING OBJECTS ANSWERS PAGE 147

COVER THE BOTTOM HALF OF THIS PAGE. Then take a look at the following 10 pictures for up to a minute. Once time is up, remove the cover from the bottom half of the page and use it to cover the top half of the page instead.

Look at the bottom group of 10 objects. Seven of them appeared in the top group, but three are different. Circle the three new objects.

PATTERN MEMORY

GRAB A PENCIL AND ERASER, and get ready to test your visual memory in a different way.
Below are four patterns on the left and four empty grids on the right. Study the first pattern for
15 seconds. Then cover it and see if you can shade in the empty grid to its right with the exact same
pattern. When you're done, uncover the original pattern to the left to see how you did. If you missed
something or the patterns didn't match, then erase the grid and try again. Repeat the same process
with the other three sets of patterns and grids.

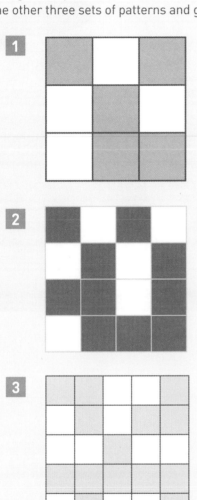

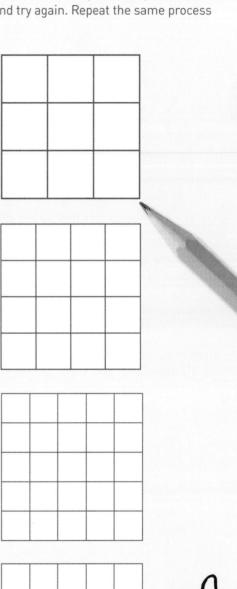

MNEMONICS

MNEMONICS (NI-MAH-NIKS) ARE HELPFUL TOOLS that can help us remember the order of a particular sequence. A common kind of mnemonic is an acronym, in which you take the first letter of the words you want to remember and turn these initials into a new word or phrase (for example, UFO, ASAP, CIA).

For example, the colors of the rainbow, in order, are red, orange, yellow, green, blue, indigo, and violet. (Indigo and violet are similar, so sometimes they are combined into just one color: purple). The colors' initials create the made-up name ROY G. BIV. That one name unlocks the order of all seven colors in your memory!

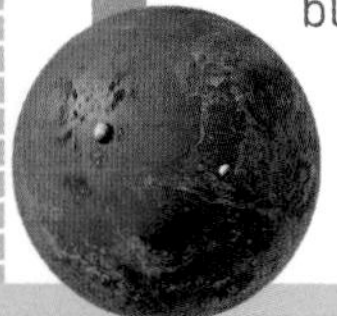

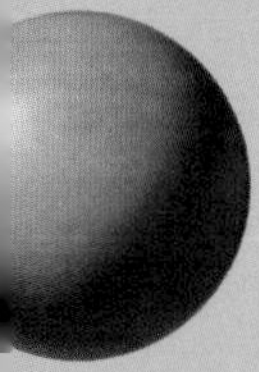

The order of the planets in the solar system from nearest to farthest from the sun is:

Mercury, Venus, Earth, Mars, Jupiter, Saturn, Uranus, Neptune

The acronym of those letters (MVEMJSUN) isn't easy to pronounce or remember—but this phrase is:

My **V**ery **E**ager **M**other **J**ust **S**lept **U**ntil **N**oon.

By remembering this one silly sentence, your brain unlocks the order of the eight planets.

Now try writing your own seven-word phrase to help you remember the colors of the rainbow. The sillier the sentence, the easier it is for your brain to remember.

ANSWER →
R

ANSWER →
O

ANSWER →
Y

ANSWER →
G

ANSWER →
B

ANSWER →
I

ANSWER →
V

[BEHIND THE BRAIN]

Every second of every day, you are exposed to a huge amount of information from your senses. Your brain must decide not only what to pay attention to, but also what is important enough to remember. If an experience triggers a strong emotional reaction, your brain considers it more important and tends to remember it. Luckily, funny things trigger an emotional response, too. When you hear or read a funny phrase, your brain will automatically rank it as more memorable than a less funny phrase.

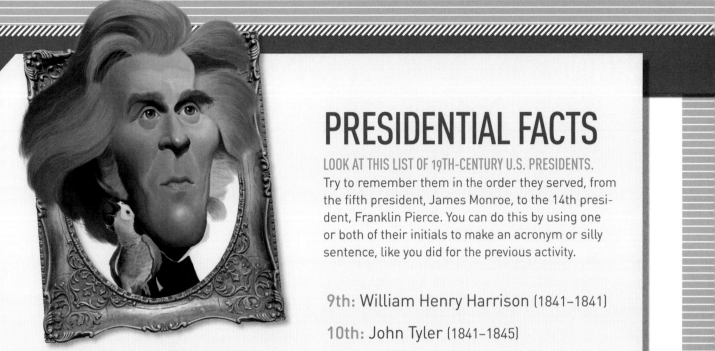

PRESIDENTIAL FACTS

LOOK AT THIS LIST OF 19TH-CENTURY U.S. PRESIDENTS.
Try to remember them in the order they served, from the fifth president, James Monroe, to the 14th president, Franklin Pierce. You can do this by using one or both of their initials to make an acronym or silly sentence, like you did for the previous activity.

5th: James Monroe (1817–1825)

6th: John Quincy Adams (1825–1829)

7th: Andrew Jackson (1829–1837)

8th: Martin Van Buren (1837–1841)

9th: William Henry Harrison (1841–1841)

10th: John Tyler (1841–1845)

11th: James K. Polk (1845–1849)

12th: Zachary Tayler (1849–1850)

13th: Millard Fillmore (1850–1853)

14th: Franklin Pierce (1853–1857)

Study the list for as long as you think you need, then cover it. Now try to write each president's name in the correct position below.

ANSWER →
5th

ANSWER →
6th

ANSWER →
7th

ANSWER →
8th

ANSWER →
9th

ANSWER →
10th

ANSWER →
11th

ANSWER →
12th

ANSWER →
13th

ANSWER →
14th

PRESIDENTS:

Andrew Jackson	John Quincy Adams	Zachary Tayler
Franklin Pierce	John Tyler	William Henry Harrison
James K. Polk	Martin Van Buren	
James Monroe	Millard Fillmore	

STATE CAPITALS

LOOK AT THE FOLLOWING LIST OF U.S. STATES AND THEIR CAPITALS. You might already know some of them from school but spend as much time as you need to memorize the remaining ones.

When you are ready, cover the left-hand table. Fill in the missing states and capitals in the incomplete table on the right. The first letter of each missing name is given to help jog your memory.

STATE	STATE CAPITAL
Alabama	Montgomery
Delaware	Dover
Maryland	Annapolis
Vermont	Montpelier
Connecticut	Hartford
Kansas	Topeka
Montana	Helena
Wisconsin	Madison

STATE	STATE CAPITAL
Alabama	M_____
Delaware	D_____
M_____	Annapolis
Vermont	M_____
C_____	Hartford
K_____	Topeka
Montana	H_____
Wisconsin	M_____

WORLD CAPITALS

ANSWERS PAGE 147

DID YOU KNOW THERE ARE NEARLY 200 COUNTRIES IN THE WORLD?
Think of all the trips you could take to learn about new people, places, and cultures! Start by taking this mental journey through 16 countries and their capitals. Draw a line to join each capital to the country it is found in. An example is filled in already.

CAPITAL CITY	COUNTRY
Abu Dhabi	Argentina
Beijing	Australia
Berlin	Belgium
Brasília	Brazil
Brussels	Canada
Buenos Aires	China
Cairo	Egypt
Canberra	France
London	Germany
Mexico City	India
New Delhi	Italy
Ottawa	Japan
Paris	Mexico
Rome	United Arab Emirates
Tokyo	United Kingdom
Washington, D.C.	United States

CONTINENTAL CONFUSION ANSWERS PAGE 147

THE MAP BELOW SHOWS THE SEVEN CONTINENTS OF THE WORLD. Draw a line between each country listed below and the continent where it is located on the map. There is an example shown to get you started.

STATE YOUR LOCATION

ANSWERS PAGE 147

BELOW IS A MAP OF THE CONTINENTAL UNITED STATES (meaning Hawaii and Alaska are not included). Twelve of the states have not been labeled. Complete the map by placing each of the states listed below in its correct location.

ARIZONA

CALIFORNIA

COLORADO

FLORIDA

IOWA

MAINE

MONTANA

NEW YORK

NORTH CAROLINA

OREGON

TEXAS

WISCONSIN

ANSWER →
A:

ANSWER →
B:

ANSWER →
C:

ANSWER →
D:

ANSWER →
E:

ANSWER →
F:

ANSWER →
G:

ANSWER →
H:

ANSWER →
I:

ANSWER →
J:

ANSWER →
K:

ANSWER →
L:

ANIMAL ANTICS ANSWERS PAGE 147

MANY COUNTRIES HAVE A NATIONAL ANIMAL. Some are official; others have just become associated with that particular country over the years. Draw a line between each of the 10 animals pictured below and the country it represents.

Australia

China

India

Japan

Kenya

New Zealand

Russia

Spain

United Kingdom

United States

1. KANGAROO

2. KIWI

3. BULL

4. BALD EAGLE

5. BEAR

6. CARP

7. BULLDOG

8. ELEPHANT

9. LION

10. GIANT PANDA

WORLD LANGUAGES

THERE ARE SOME 7,000 SPOKEN LANGUAGES IN THE WORLD.
About a third are spoken by a very small number of people, while others are widely spoken across the globe. Can you guess which language is the most widely spoken? [The answer is below.]

The words below all mean "Hello" in different languages. Some of them look similar; they may have originated from the same parent language. Study the table to the right to memorize which word belongs with which language.

LANGUAGE	WORD
Chinese	Ni Hao
French	Bonjour
German	Hallo
Hebrew	Shalom
Italian	Ciao
Japanese	Konnichiwa
Persian	Salam
Spanish	Hola

When you're done, cover the table. Then draw a line between each word below and its matching language.

Chinese

French

German

Hebrew

Italian

Japanese

Persian

Spanish

Shalom

Ciao

Bonjour

Konnichiwa

Ni Hao

Hola

Hallo

Salam

[BEHIND THE BRAIN]

Some of the words in the table were likely easier to remember than others. If a word was familiar to you, or easy to pronounce because it was similar to the English word "Hello," your brain had less new information to learn, which made it easier to remember.

MANDARIN CHINESE IS THE MOST WIDELY SPOKEN LANGUAGE IN THE WORLD. (ENGLISH COMES IN SECOND.)

COIN COLLATION

IN SOME SPORTS, SUCH AS FOOTBALL OR TENNIS, a coin toss is a common random method used to make decisions at the start of the match, such as which team plays first or starts on which side of the field. If the coin shows heads, Team A wins. If the coin shows tails, Team B wins.

A coin toss is a considered a fair way of making a choice between two options. Why? Two sides of the coin = two options. But what if you wanted to conduct an experiment to make sure that was true? If you toss a coin only twice, you might get the same result both times. To get useful results, you need to do the same experiment lots of times and look at the overall results. This is how scientists conduct experiments in the real world.

For this exercise, you will toss a coin 20 times. Write down in the table below whether it comes up as heads or tails each time. Before you start, make a guess what your tallies will be.

TOSS: Heads (H) or Tails (T)

1	2	3	4	5	6	7	8	9	10

11	12	13	14	15	16	17	18	19	20

ESTIMATE:

H	T

TOTAL:

H	T

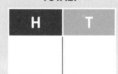

How did your totals compare with your estimates?

Chances are that you got about 10 heads, and about 10 tails. This tells you that the likelihood of getting either heads or tails is even—or in other words, the probability of both heads and tails is the same.

Each coin toss is completely independent from the previous one and next one. Just because you might get five heads in a row doesn't mean that your sixth toss will be heads, too. But because the probability is the same for heads and tails, your overall results in a series will likely have roughly the same number of heads and tails.

ILLUSION PATTERNS

ANSWER PAGE 148

GRAB A PEN OR MARKER (WITH STRONG, DARK INK) and a ruler or other straight-edged object. You'll use these tools to turn the concentric circles below into optical illusions.

Draw a square or rectangle centered over the top left circle. What do you see? It should look like the lines of your square or rectangle bend in toward the center of the circle.

Now, experiment with making more illusions using the other circles. You can draw a large rectangle that joins two sets of circles, or experiment with shapes with more—or fewer—than four sides.

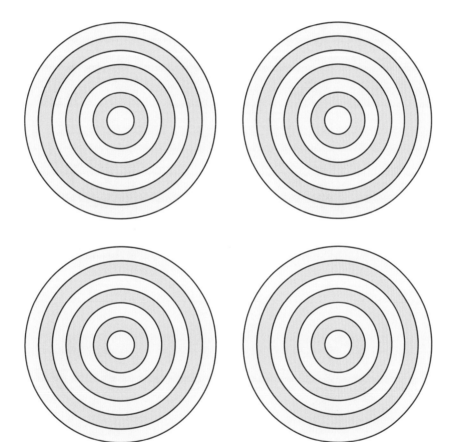

Do some shapes work better than others? Do the lines appear to bend more if they pass through certain parts of a circle? As you try different approaches, you'll learn what works best in this type of illusion.

[BEHIND THE BRAIN]

Your brain interprets each set of circles as a 3D "tunnel" and perceives the circles at the center to be farthest away. When you then draw straight lines over the circles, your brain assumes they are bending along with the curve of the "tunnel."

WHO IS NEW?

ANSWERS PAGE 148

OUR HUMAN BRAINS HAVE EVOLVED TO BE PRETTY GOOD AT RECOGNIZING FACES—so much so, in fact, that we sometimes "see" them where they don't exist, such as in a cloud, the bark of a tree, or the surface of the moon. Cover the bottom half of this page, then take a look at the faces on the top half for no more than a minute.

Next, remove the cover from the bottom half of the page and use it to cover the top half of the page instead. Then circle the faces you have seen before. (Five faces are the same.)

NAMES AND FACES

ANSWERS PAGE 148

Cover the bottom half of this page and take a look at the following eight people. Each person's name appears below their picture. Study the pairings and try to remember the name that goes with each person.

| Liam | Chris | Nicky | William | Ava | Sergio | Isabella | Olivia |

Next, remove the cover from the bottom half of the page and use it to cover the top half of the page instead. In the group below, all eight people are the same, but four of the names are wrong. Circle the correct names and cross out the incorrect ones.

| Sergio | Isabella | Nicky | William | Chris | Ava | Olivia | Liam |

[BEHIND THE BRAIN]

Are you one of those people who always remembers everyone's name, or do you seem to totally forget a name as soon as you've heard it? The secret of remembering a name is mostly to pay attention. This means making a conscious effort to remember it. Simply repeating the name back can help. You can either do this in your head or, if it's appropriate, you could say something with the person's name in it, like, "Nice to meet you, Martha." If you don't do this, you might find you forget the name really quickly.

MISSING SHAPES

COVER THE "RECALL" GRID ON THE BOTTOM. Then study the "Memorize" grid on the top for a minute. Try to remember the position of each shape on the grid.

MEMORIZE

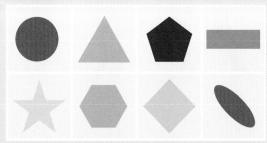

Next, remove the cover from the "Recall" grid and use it to cover the "Memorize" grid. The "Recall" grid has several blanks. Draw the missing shapes in their proper position on the "Recall" grid. (Don't worry about the colors; focus on the shapes.)

RECALL

MISSING WORDS

COVER THE "RECALL" GRID ON THE BOTTOM. Then study the "Memorize" grid on the top for a minute. Try to remember the words in the "Memorize" grid.

MEMORIZE

Elephant	Dream
Crayon	Orange
Event	Computer
Lemon	Mail
Mouse	Vacation

Next, remove the cover from the "Recall" grid and use it to cover the "Memorize" grid. See if you can write the missing words in the "Recall" grid in the same positions they were in originally.

RECALL

Elep _____	D _____
Cr_____	Or_____
Eve_____	C_____
Le_____	Ma_____
_____	V_____

HOUSEHOLD OBJECTS

COVER THE BOTTOM HALF OF THE PAGE. Then spend up to a minute studying the top map of a house. Pay attention to where each object is.

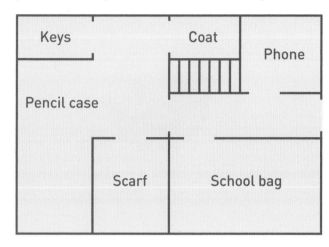

Next, remove the cover from the bottom half of the page and use it to cover the top half of the page instead. Look at the list of objects below. Write the name of each object into its proper location on the bottom map.

COAT   PENCIL CASE

PHONE   SCARF

KEYS   SCHOOL BAG

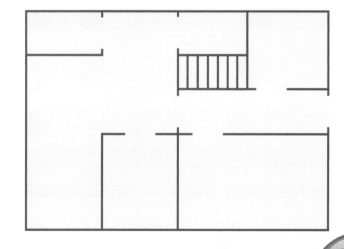

[BEHIND THE BRAIN]

Do you ever forget where you put things in real life, too? The secret to remembering where you put something is to pay attention. Each time you put something down, say to yourself where you are putting it. ("I am putting my phone on the kitchen table.") You can say it out loud or in your head; both ensure that you are paying conscious attention. Repeating it also helps strengthen the memory. Or imagine walking through your house. As you visualize the different places where you might have placed something, you might suddenly remember where you left what you're looking for!

CIRCLE LINK ANSWER PAGE 148

Draw horizontal and vertical lines to join the circles into pairs, so that each pair contains one purple circle and one aqua blue circle. Lines can't cross each other, and they also can't cross over another circle. Every circle must be part of exactly **one** pair.

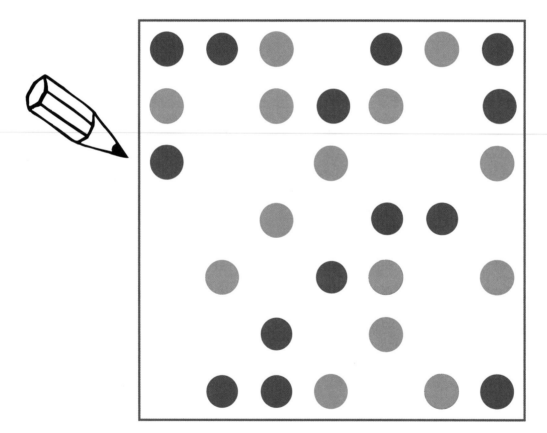

TIME STARTED	TIME ENDED	TOTAL TIME

NUMBER DARTS

ANSWER PAGE 148

Add together one number from the outer ring, one from the middle ring, and one from the inner ring so that their sum equals the first total below. Repeat the process so that your sums match the second, then the third total. You can reuse a number for different totals.

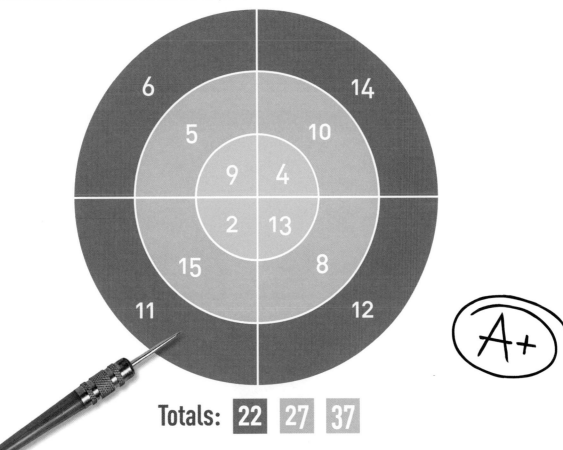

Totals: 22 27 37

TIME STARTED

TIME ENDED

TOTAL TIME

CHAPTER **FOUR**
NUMBER SKILLS

Numbers are part of life everywhere on Earth. Mathematics is the only language shared by people worldwide, regardless of culture, nationality, or religion. Whether we're adding up the cost of a basket of groceries or figuring out how to divide up a cake at a party, we're using number skills to do it. And math isn't just part of human life—it explains how everything works, from the tiniest atom to the biggest planet.

Even though math is part of everything around us, some people find it confusing and intimidating. But your brain is capable of far more number skills than you might realize. Read on to learn how your brain tackles math challenges—then try some for yourself!

→

COUNTING **CHALLENGE**

SEVERAL COPIES OF THE TREE SHOWN IN GREEN HAVE BEEN PLACED ON TOP OF ONE ANOTHER in the yellow picture below. Can you count how many trees there are in the yellow picture?

HINT: Look for a unique feature, such as the point of a tree, and count just that feature. Or, try drawing over the outline of each tree, one by one.

[BEHIND THE BRAIN]

This puzzle probably looked more complex at first sight than it actually was. Why?

Most of the time, your brain works out the basics of what you're looking at without any conscious effort. That's why you can recognize faces, for example, without having to stop and think, "That's a round object. If it has eyes, nose, and a mouth, then it's probably a face." Your brain does this analysis automatically. But, your brain has no experience with processing unusual images, like the one above. You're left to do all the untangling of the image yourself, which makes it seem more complex by comparison.

NUMBERS IN YOUR NOGGIN

HERE'S ONE THING YOU CAN COUNT ON: YOU USE NUMBERS EVERY DAY, FROM KEEPING TRACK OF HOW LONG YOUR HOMEWORK WILL TAKE TO ESTIMATING THE NUMBER OF EMPTY SEATS AT THE MOVIE THEATER. HOW DOES YOUR BRAIN TACKLE MATH?

MENTAL MATH

Some people struggle to remember their times tables—but others can ponder how mathematical laws control the movements of the stars and planets, much like Albert Einstein could. What's unique about the brain of a math genius?

Scientists have long wondered whether math experts use a different part of the brain than the rest of us while thinking about the mathematical mysteries of the universe. But a 2016 study that compared the brains of professional mathematicians to those of experts in other fields showed something unexpected: The mathematicians weren't using some new surprising part of the brain at all. Instead, they were using the same brain area that toddlers use when they're learning to count!

Scientists think that humans, and even some other animals, are born with a natural number sense. And this research hints that whether you're an infant or Einstein, the brain uses the same network when it thinks about math.

IT'S ALL ABOUT ATTITUDE

When you look at a math problem, do you feel a sense of dread—or does the challenge give you a rush of excitement? New research shows that how good a person is at math may simply have a lot to do with attitude.

In 2018, researchers collected questionnaires from 240 kids between the ages of seven and 10 to gather information about their level of anxiety

toward math. The scientists also measured math ability with a test of math word problems and facts about arithmetic. Then they had kids solve math problems while inside a brain scanner. The experiment showed that children who had positive attitudes toward math had more activity in the hippocampus, an area of the brain that helps with learning and memory. The hippocampus stayed quiet in kids who had a negative attitude toward math.

This experiment shows that a positive attitude toward math may help the brain use the powers of the hippocampus to recall learned math skills and help solve problems. So, the next time you feel intimidated by a math problem, try giving yourself a pep talk—because if you believe you can do it, science shows you really can!

MOST PEOPLE CAN **HOLD A SHORT SERIES OF NUMBERS**—SUCH AS A PHONE NUMBER—IN THEIR HEAD FOR ABOUT **7 SECONDS.** FOR **LETTERS,** THE AVERAGE IS AROUND **9 SECONDS.**

GIRLS VS. BOYS

It's a stereotype that's been around for decades—boys are just better at math than girls. But is it true? In 2008, scientists decided to find out once and for all. They gathered the most recent math scores from standardized tests in 10 states across the United States for kids in grades two through 11. This gave the researchers a huge amount of data, or information, to study.

The researchers compared how boys performed on math tests to how girls performed. And the verdict? There was no difference. Science shows the idea that boys have an innate math ability is nothing more than a myth.

FRUIT FOR THOUGHT

ANSWERS PAGE 148

EACH FRUIT IS A STAND-IN FOR A PARTICULAR NUMBER. Can you figure out the value of each item of fruit, given the following picture equations? Write each fruit's value in the boxes below.

1

apple + banana = 7

banana + orange = 6

orange + apple = 5

apple = ANSWER →

banana = ANSWER →

orange = ANSWER →

In this second puzzle, a fruit appears more than once in each calculation.

2

pineapple + pineapple + strawberry + strawberry = apple

apple − pineapple + pineapple = pineapple

apple + strawberry + strawberry + pineapple = 10

pineapple = ANSWER →

apple = ANSWER →

strawberry = ANSWER →

BALANCED DIET

ANSWERS PAGE 148

EACH TYPE OF FRUIT IN THE PUZZLE BELOW HAS A DIFFERENT WEIGHT. By examining the following three balances, can you figure out which is the heaviest type of fruit, and which is the lightest type of fruit? (For the purpose of this puzzle, ignore the distance of a fruit from the fulcrum—or center—of the scale.)

1

HEAVIEST FRUIT→

LIGHTEST FRUIT→

A healthy diet includes fruits AND vegetables! Solve this trickier puzzle by figuring out which of the four kinds of vegetables below is the heaviest and the lightest.

2

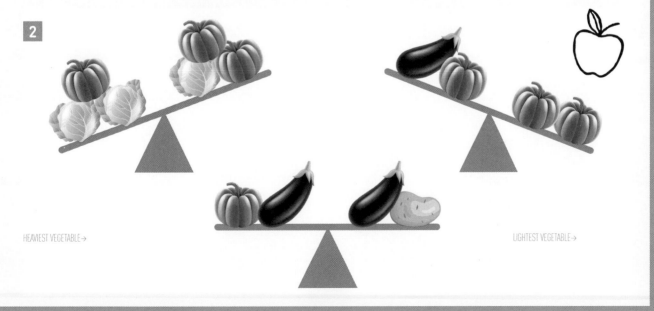

HEAVIEST VEGETABLE→

LIGHTEST VEGETABLE→

NUMBER PYRAMID

ANSWER PAGE 148

COMPLETE THE NUMBER PYRAMID by writing a number in each empty square. Every square in the pyramid must contain a value exactly equal to the total of the two squares immediately beneath it. Start on the right-hand side, then work up and down the puzzle until you've filled in every box.

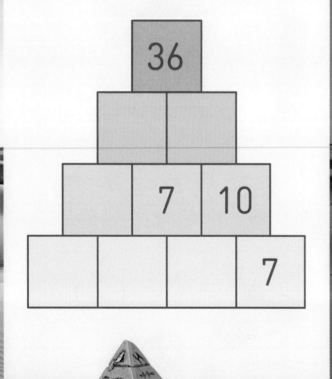

ARITHMETIC SQUARE

ANSWER PAGE 148

PLACE THE NUMBERS 1 TO 9 ONLY ONE TIME EACH INTO the nine empty green boxes, so that each one of the calculations equals the totals given at both the vertical and horizontal ends of the puzzle. Some squares are already solved for you to get you started.

1	+		+		=	10
×		+		×		
	+	7	+		=	18
+		+		+		
	×		+		=	21
=		=		=		
5		18		41		

FUTOSHIKI
ANSWER PAGE 148

PLACE A NUMBER FROM 1 TO 5 INTO EACH EMPTY SQUARE in the grid so that no number repeats in any row or column. Some pairs of squares have greater-than and less-than arrows between them. These arrows always point to the square with the lower of the two numbers.

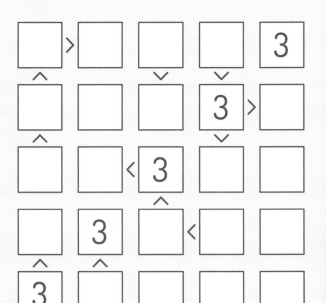

KAKURO
ANSWER PAGE 149

THIS PUZZLE IS ARRANGED LIKE A CROSSWORD. It has horizontal and vertical "runs" of white squares. Place a number from 1 to 9 into each white square, so that each run of numbers adds up to the sum given at the start of that run. You can use a number only once in each run. But you may repeat a number within a row or column if it appears in separate runs.

One of the runs is solved for you. (5+3+1 = 9, the number given at the start of the run.)

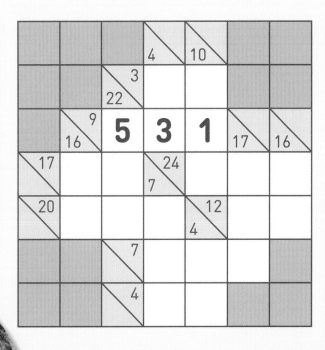

BRAIN CHAINS   ANSWERS PAGE 149

CAN YOU SOLVE THESE BRAIN CHAINS WITHOUT WRITING ANY CALCULATIONS?

Start at the number on the far left of each chain. Follow the arrows and perform each of the calculations in sequence—all in your head. Write your result in the empty box at the end of each chain.

The chains get progressively trickier as you go.

| 19 | +6 | -17 | +1 | ×5 | ÷9 | RESULT |

| 5 | +7 | ÷2 | ×9 | -3 | +12 | RESULT |

| 44 | -6 | ×2 | ÷4 | +11 | ÷2 | RESULT |

| 34 | +26 | -19 | +29 | -15 | ÷11 | RESULT |

[BEHIND THE BRAIN]

You probably found that it was more difficult to work out these brain chains in your head compared to writing them down. Once you started working out the result of the next step, you likely found yourself forgetting the number you just solved for. The reason is that your brain has a very limited memory for temporarily storing the results of calculations; it can hold only about five to seven digits. The more difficult the equation you are solving, the more likely you are to lose track of your numbers.

FLOATING NUMBERS

ANSWERS PAGE 149

EACH OF THESE BALLOONS HAS A DIFFERENT TOTAL WRITTEN ON IT. Can you figure out how to form each of the given totals, adding together only combinations of the six numbers given? (For example, you could form a total of 12 by pairing the 4 and 8 balloons.)

10

6

8

11

4

9

TOTALS:

16 = ANSWER →

22 = ANSWER →

26 = ANSWER →

32 = ANSWER →

40 = ANSWER →

CALCUDOKU CHALLENGE ANSWERS PAGE 149

PLACE A NUMBER FROM 1 TO 4 IN EACH SQUARE, SO THAT NO NUMBER REPEATS IN ANY ROW OR COLUMN.

The numbers in each bold-lined jigsaw puzzle piece must add up to the small number printed at the top left of each piece. (If a puzzle piece has only one square, you know automatically which number you need!)

Here is an example to show you how it works.

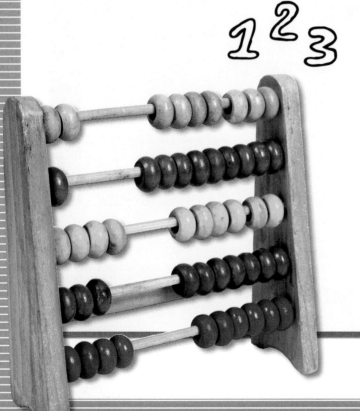

CALCUDOKU + - × ÷

ANSWERS PAGE 149

IN THESE CALCUDOKU PUZZLES, YOU WILL NEED TO ADD, SUBTRACT, MULTIPLY, OR DIVIDE the numbers in each jigsaw puzzle piece to equal the total given. For subtraction and division, start with the largest number in the puzzle piece and then subtract or divide by the other number.

Here is an example to show you how it works.

A QUESTION OF AGE
ANSWERS PAGE 149

THREE SISTERS ARE COMPARING THEIR AGES.
- Cecilia is two years older than Isabel.
- When Isabel is a year older, she will be exactly half Maria's current age.
- Maria is three years older than Cecilia.

How old is each girl?

Isabel is ANSWER →   **Cecilia is** ANSWER →   **Maria is** ANSWER →

SHOPPING PROBLEM
ANSWERS PAGE 149

THE SUPERMARKET IS CHARGING THESE PRICES FOR FOUR COMMON GROCERY ITEMS:

Cheese: $1.50   Milk: $2.25   Butter: $3.50   Juice: $2.75

Use the prices to answer the following questions.

1) If you buy both milk and butter, how much change would you get from a $10 bill?
ANSWER →

2) Which is cheaper: Two milks and one butter, or three cheeses and one juice?
ANSWER →

3) You buy one each of all four items above, plus you spend another $7.50 on other products. In your wallet, you have several $1, $2, $5, and $10 bills. What is the **smallest** number of bills you can use to pay for your shopping? (You don't use any coins.)
ANSWER →

TIME PUZZLES

ANSWERS PAGE 149

TRY THESE TIME-BASED CALCULATIONS.

1) It is 9:00 a.m. In four hours, you must leave to go shopping. At what time do you need to leave?

ANSWER →

2) You ate breakfast at 8:00 a.m. and your evening meal at 5:00 p.m. If you ate your lunch exactly halfway between these two times, at what time did you eat your lunch?

ANSWER →

3) What time is it when it is halfway through the second half of the day? Assume that a day starts and ends at midnight.

ANSWER →

TIME ZONE PROBLEMS

ANSWERS PAGE 149

EARTH IS DIVIDED INTO 24 TIME ZONES. Take a mental trip around the globe with these time zone travel teasers.

When it is 12 p.m. in winter in Washington, D.C., it is this time in these six locations:

- 7 a.m. in Hawaii, United States
- 9 a.m. in California, United States
- 5 p.m. in London, United Kingdom
- 6 p.m. in Paris, France
- 2 a.m. tomorrow in Tokyo, Japan
- 4 a.m. tomorrow in Sydney, Australia

1) If it is 3 p.m. in London, what time is it in California?

ANSWER →

2) When it is noon in Hawaii, what time is it in Sydney?

ANSWER →

3) The flight from Paris to Tokyo lasts 11 hours and 30 minutes. If you leave Paris at 9 a.m., what time will it be in Tokyo when you land?

ANSWER →

DICE FACES ANSWERS PAGE 149

A STANDARD DIE HAS SIX FACES. Each face has a different number of dots from one to six.

They look like this:

1) If you add up the six different sides of the dice, what is the total?

ANSWER →

2) The opposite sides of a die always add up to seven. (For example, if you see two dots on the front side, there will be five dots on the back side. 2+5=7.) If you add up the opposite sides of these four dice, what total do you get?

ANSWER →

3) Some of the spots have rubbed off these dice! Remembering that the 2, 3, and 6 have two possible appearances, depending on whether they are rotated or not, answer these questions:

A) How many of these dice could possibly be showing a 6?

ANSWER →

B) How many could possibly be showing a 3?

ANSWER →

C) What is the minimum possible total of these five dice?

ANSWER →

D) What is the maximum possible total for these five dice?

ANSWER →

DOT-TO-DOT DECISIONS

ANSWER PAGE 150

JOIN THE DOTS IN THIS PUZZLE IN INCREASING NUMERICAL ORDER, USING STRAIGHT LINES. Start from 3 and work your way upward, drawing a line to 6, then 7, then 9, and so on.

HINT: All of the numbers are multiples of either 3 or 7. You can use your times tables to help figure out which number comes next.

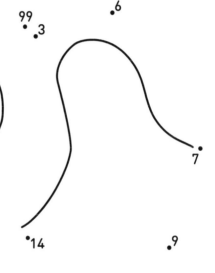
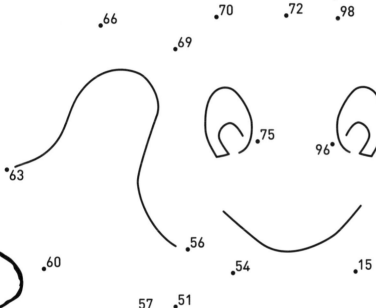

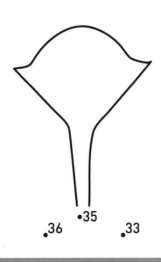
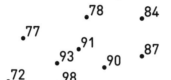

.81
.78
.84
.77
.91
.87
.93
.90
.98
.66
.70
.72
.99
.6
.69
.3
.75
.96
.63
.7
.56
.14
.60
.54
.15
.9
.57 .51
.18
.12
.49
.21
.48
.24
.45
.39
.35
.30
.27
.42
.36
.33
.28

ODD ONE OUT

ANSWERS PAGE 150

THERE IS A NUMBER THAT DOESN'T BELONG IN EACH OF THE FOLLOWING SETS. Can you spot the number that is not like the others in each set, and say why?

A | 4 | 12 | 24 | 15 | 96 | 44 | 18 |

ANSWER →

B | 18 | 27 | 3 | 36 | 15 | 16 | 21 |

ANSWER →

C | 82 | 50 | 19 | 37 | 64 | 55 | 73 |

ANSWER →

HINT:
For C and D, think about the digits making up each number.

D | 82 | 70 | 56 | 91 | 42 | 63 | 40 |

ANSWER →

[BEHIND THE BRAIN]

Your brain is always on the lookout for patterns in your day-to-day life. For example, when you're learning to ride a bike, your brain notices the pattern of movements that keeps you from falling off! For the number sequences above, once your brain figured out a pattern, it was then able to apply that pattern more easily and more quickly the next time. Your brain locks these patterns away for future use, so you can make a sensible guess when you next encounter a similar situation.

SEQUENCE SOLVING ANSWERS PAGE 150

EACH OF THE FOLLOWING SETS OF NUMBERS FOLLOWS A PARTICULAR SEQUENCE—except for one number that does not belong. Identify the sequences and then cross out the incorrect number. The first one is done for you as an example.

A 3 5 7 ~~8~~ 9 11 13 15

Once the 8 is crossed out, a sequence in which each number is two larger than the previous number is created.

B 6 7 8 10 12 14 16 18

C 35 32 29 26 24 23 20 17

D 5 6 8 11 15 18 20 26

MULTIPLICATION SEARCH

ANSWERS PAGE 150

ANSWER EACH OF THESE MULTIPLICATION PROBLEMS. Then find the completed problem in the word search grid. Problems can be written in any direction, including diagonally, and may read either forward or backward.

One problem is solved and highlighted for you as an example: 4 × 10 = 40.

- ☐ 1 × ___ = 5
- ☐ ___ × 3 = 6
- ☐ 2 × ___ = 10
- ☐ 2 × 8 = ___
- ☐ ___ × 12 = 24
- ☐ 3 × ___ = 15
- ☐ 3 × 7 = ___
- ☐ ___ × 8 = 24
- ☐ 4 × 10 = **40**
- ☐ 4 × ___ = 44
- ☐ ___ × 4 = 20
- ☐ ___ × 7 = 35
- ☐ ___ × 6 = 36
- ☐ 7 × ___ = 7
- ☐ 7 × ___ = 63
- ☐ ___ × 7 = 56
- ☐ 9 × ___ = 36
- ☐ 10 × 3 = ___

=	×	3	0	4	=	0	1	×	4	6	3	=	5	0	3
6	2	×	0	6	0	×	2	5	3	×	6	3	6	1	2
5	×	8	5	6	=	3	3	=	2	3	=	×	×	0	7
=	2	=	2	=	1	2	3	3	=	7	×	1	3	×	=
=	4	2	=	5	=	5	6	6	×	=	6	=	×	3	8
=	1	4	×	6	1	=	×	5	=	0	5	0	2	=	1
5	×	=	2	=	9	6	7	5	4	1	=	9	4	3	1
3	=	6	5	×	=	6	0	4	4	2	7	0	2	0	6
4	3	×	7	=	1	=	0	1	=	5	×	2	1	×	7
4	3	6	5	×	=	2	=	1	9	5	8	3	2	2	1
4	0	2	=	4	×	5	=	4	=	=	5	×	×	3	×
=	6	1	6	=	3	×	2	7	5	×	1	8	8	×	5
1	=	7	1	8	0	1	=	2	1	2	=	=	5	7	=
1	×	1	7	3	5	1	5	4	=	1	7	=	×	=	5
×	=	=	=	2	×	1	1	2	6	=	0	5	×	2	4
4	6	2	=	7	9	×	4	=	3	6	2	4	5	1	=

NUMBER TRIANGLES

ANSWERS PAGE 150

EACH SIDE OF THIS TRIANGLE CONTAINS A MULTIPLICATION EQUATION.
The factors in the circles multiply together to equal the product
in the box. Complete each equation by writing the correct number in each empty circle.

The first one is done for you as an example.

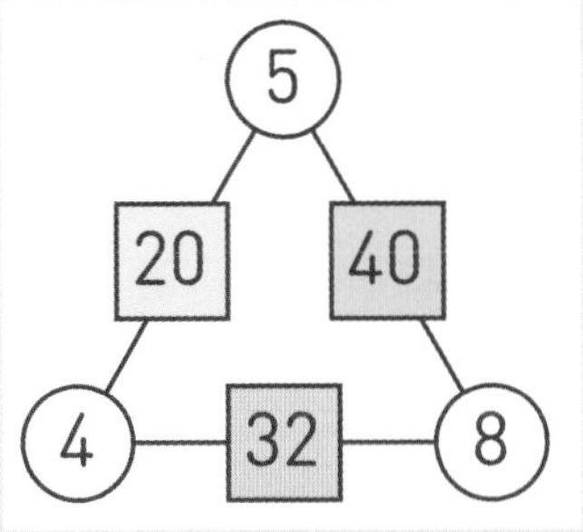

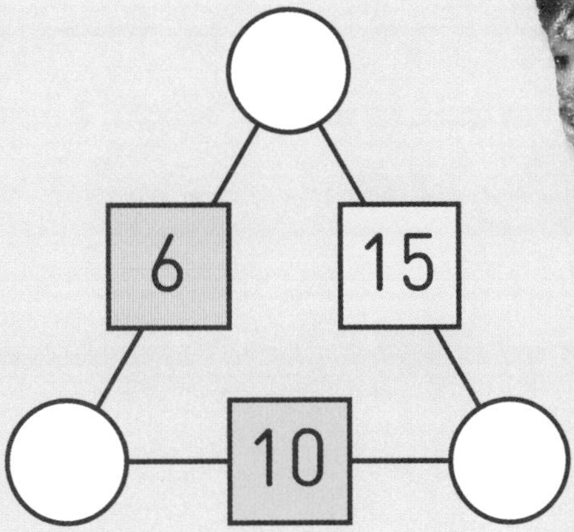

Example:
- 5
- 20   40
- 4   32   8

1
- (empty)
- 6   15
- (empty)   10   (empty)

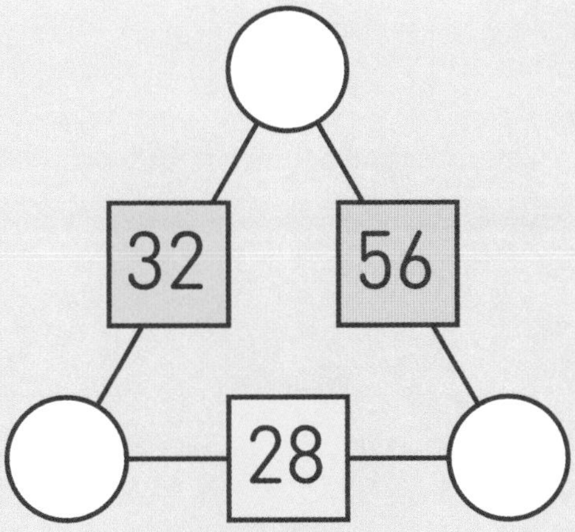

2
- (empty)
- 32   56
- (empty)   28   (empty)

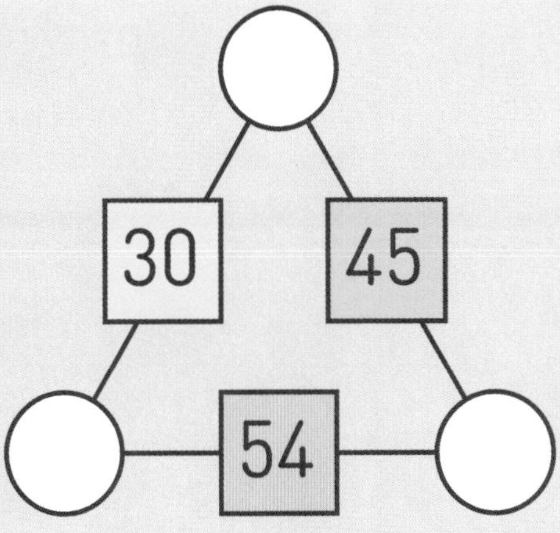

3
- (empty)
- 30   45
- (empty)   54   (empty)

CIRCLE LINK ANSWER PAGE 150

Draw horizontal and vertical lines to join the circles into pairs, so that each pair contains one blue circle and one orange circle. Lines can't cross each other, and they also can't cross over another circle. Every circle must be part of exactly one pair.

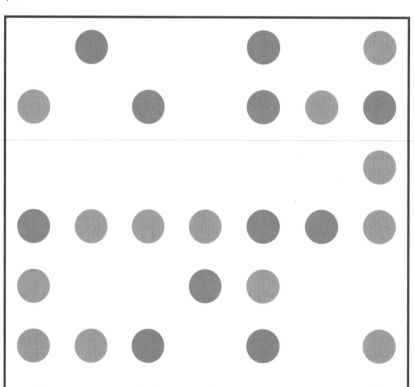

TIME STARTED

TIME ENDED

TOTAL TIME

NUMBER DARTS ANSWERS PAGE 150

Add together one number from the outer ring, one from the middle ring, and one from the inner ring so that their sum equals the first total below. Repeat the process so that your sums match the second, then the third total. For example, you could form a total of 12 by adding 3 from the inner ring, 4 from the middle ring, and 5 from the outer ring.

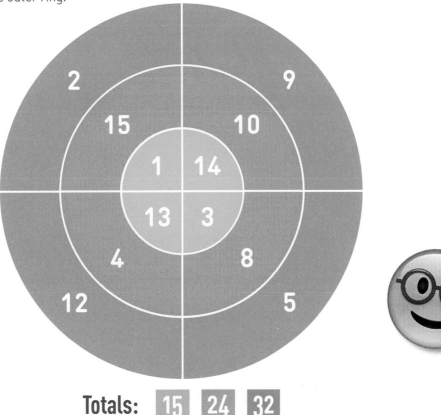

Totals: 15 24 32

TIME STARTED	TIME ENDED	TOTAL TIME

CHAPTER **FIVE**
CREATIVITY

When you think of intelligence, you might picture acing a history test or solving math problems in your head. But there's another type of intelligence: creativity. Creativity, the ability to come up with new ideas, isn't as easy to measure as the ability to memorize facts or divide fractions. But it's a type of mental might that helps us solve problems in the world around us.

Where does creativity come from? And what's happening in our brains when we are dreaming up new ideas? Scientists are just beginning to answer these questions. Read on to learn a little of what they've discovered—then test your own creativity with the puzzles in this chapter!

→

COLORING CHALLENGE

GRAB A HANDFUL OF COLORED PENS OR PENCILS AND START COLORING. Use one color per bordered area and as many different colors as you like. There are no right or wrong ways to do this puzzle; just let your creative juices flow!

[BEHIND THE BRAIN]

Some people don't consider themselves creative. But the truth is that everyone is deeply creative every day of their lives! Our brain makes sense of our world by coming up with creative explanations that join together all of the things we observe and know into a sensible narrative of our lives. For example, when you recall a memory of a specific event, you're actually calling up a lot of small memories and joining them together with your built-in storytelling skills.

For the picture above, it was easy to be creative because you didn't have to stop and think about what to do. Instead, you let your brain's natural creativity take over. This puzzle shows just how creative we all can be, if only we let ourselves start!

IMAGINATION AND INSPIRATION

EVERYONE HAS EXPERIENCED THAT SUDDEN FLASH OF CREATIVITY WHEN THE ANSWER TO A PROBLEM THEY'VE BEEN STRUGGLING WITH SUDDENLY BECOMES CLEAR. HERE'S WHAT HAPPENS WHEN THE MIND GOES FROM *SAY WHAT?* TO *AHA!*

CREATIVE CRANIUM

Do the brains of highly creative people look different from the brains of people who aren't as creative? That's what scientists have wondered, and in 2018, they tested a group of about 160 volunteers; they monitored their brain activity while asking them to think of out-of-the-box uses for a set of common objects, including a brick, a cup, and a rope.

Then scientists compared the brain activity of creative people, who performed well on the task, with that of people who didn't. They found that when the creative people tried to come up with new ways to use the objects, three different areas of their brain lit up at once. Normally, these areas of the brain don't work together. But the study showed that creative people have brain cells that connect these areas, showing that the ability to be creative may be found in the brain's network of connections.

INSIDE A RAPPER'S BRAIN

Musicians, athletes, and artists call it flow: the mental state they enter when they lose themselves in what they're doing and perform almost without thinking. To get a deeper look into what's going on during this state, scientists studied the brains of 12 professional rappers. While their brains were being scanned, the artists listened to an instrumental track. First, they rapped memorized lyrics. Then they freestyled, a type of rapping in which artists have to improvise lyrics and rhythm on the fly.

The researchers found that when the rappers began freestyling, their brain activity looked totally different. The parts of the brain responsible for self-monitoring and editing turned off. In other words, the parts of the brain that edit what we say became silent when the rappers entered the flow state. To be creative, the research hints, we have to let go of control, and allow our brains to come up with new ideas.

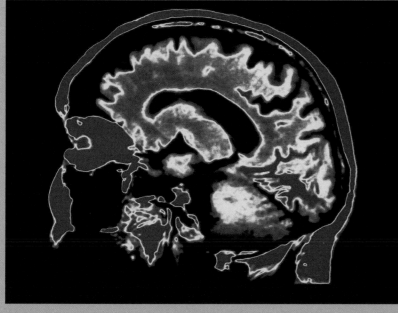

PICTURE THIS

If you ask most people to think of a sandy beach or a dark forest, they immediately form a picture in their mind. But what if they couldn't imagine? Some scientists think that's the case for people with aphantasia, a condition that prevents people from visualizing mental images. Some people are that way from birth; others lose the ability after suffering brain damage.

Scientists are just beginning to study aphantasia, and some are not sure it exists at all. But early studies have shown that there are brain differences between people who report having the condition and people who don't. When asked to visualize something, most people use areas of the brain known to be involved in processing images. But those who report having aphantasia instead use brain areas associated with planning and controlling behavior.

And scientists have learned one surprising thing about the condition. They initially thought that without the ability to visualize, people with aphantasia could not be creative. After all, how can you think of how to solve a problem or complete a task if you can't picture it? But instead, researchers have found that many people who report having aphantasia often have creative professions, including art, architecture, and science. Studying people with this brain condition could help scientists learn more about how creativity works in the brain.

MONSTER MATCHUP

TAKE A LOOK AT THE FOLLOWING PICTURES OF MADE-UP CREATURES. Use your creativity to name each creature. Write the name below each picture.

ANSWER →

ANSWER →

ANSWER →

ANSWER →

ANSWER →

ANSWER →

TOOL TIME

EACH OF THE TOOLS ON THIS PAGE HAS BEEN CREATED BY MERGING TWO OR MORE EXISTING TOOLS. Instead of giving them ordinary-sounding names, like "brush with a ruler for a handle," use your imagination to come up with fun, quirky names. Write the name of each new tool next to its picture.

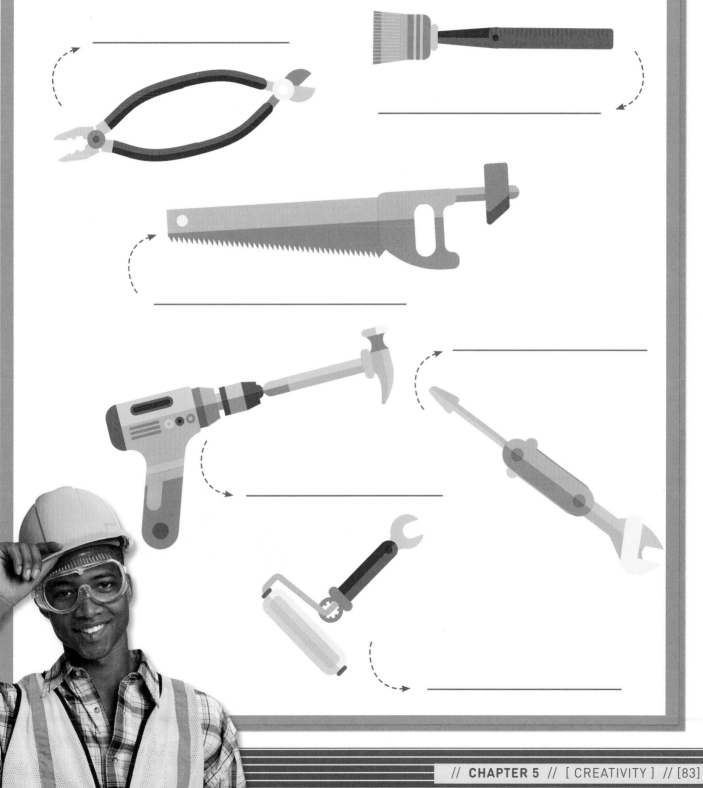

WHAT'S IN THE BOX?

PART OF EACH OF THESE CREATURES IS COVERED BY A WHITE BOX. Use your creativity to draw in what's hidden behind the box.

MYSTERIOUS SHADOWS

SOME CREATURES ARE LURKING IN THE SHADOWS; you can only see their silhouettes.
Use your imagination to draw in what each creature would look like if it were fully lit.

RHYMING COUPLETS

A RHYMING COUPLET IS A PAIR OF SENTENCES THAT:
- Are roughly the same length
- Rhyme
- Work together to express one idea

Can you come up with a second line to complete each of these couplets? You can start by choosing your last word, which has to rhyme with the last word of the first line, and then craft the rest of your sentence. There are no right or wrong answers, just your own creative expressions!

   The first couplet is completed for you as an example.

- Every day, as I eat my lunch,
  I like to hear my sandwich crunch.

- As I wander through the school,
  ANSWER →

- Twenty-five days in a row,
  ANSWER →

- Lying on the edge of sleep,
  ANSWER →

like

COMPLETE THE JOKE

HERE ARE SOME HALF-WRITTEN JOKES. It's up to you to supply either the setup line or the punchline. Again, there are no correct answers; write whatever you think would make your personal audience roar with laughter.

What do you get if you cross a dresser and a pair of scissors?
ANSWER →

Did you hear the one about the parrot with the missing leg?
ANSWER →

Why did the book feel embarrassed?
ANSWER →

QUESTION →

A TV show.

COMPLETE THE STORY

SOME OF THE WORDS ARE MISSING FROM THE FOLLOWING STORY. Fill in each blank with any word you want, as long as it matches the part of speech shown (or choose a name where shown).
Make your tale as funny or factual as you like.
• Noun: a person, place, or thing
• Verb: an action word, like "run" or "jump"
• Adjective: a word describing a noun, like "clever"
• Adverb: a word describing a verb, like "quickly"

My friend _____ [PERSON'S NAME] came to visit from _____ [PLACE NAME] last weekend.

After (s)he arrived, (s)he asked for some _____ [ADJECTIVE] _____ [NOUN],

which I didn't have. So we _____ [ADVERB] _____ [VERB] to the

_____ [NOUN] to buy some.

When we arrived, we discovered there was a big discount on

_____ [ADJECTIVE] _____ [NOUN]. My friend _____ [VERB] with excitement.

"Let's buy _____ [NOUN]!" (s)he _____ [VERB]. Since we had money

left over, we also bought _____ [ADJECTIVE] _____ [NOUN]. We

_____ [ADVERB] took our _____ [NOUN] to the register and paid with

_____ [NOUN]. We _____ [VERB] it all on the way home. We felt

_____ [ADJECTIVE] but so _____ [ADJECTIVE]!

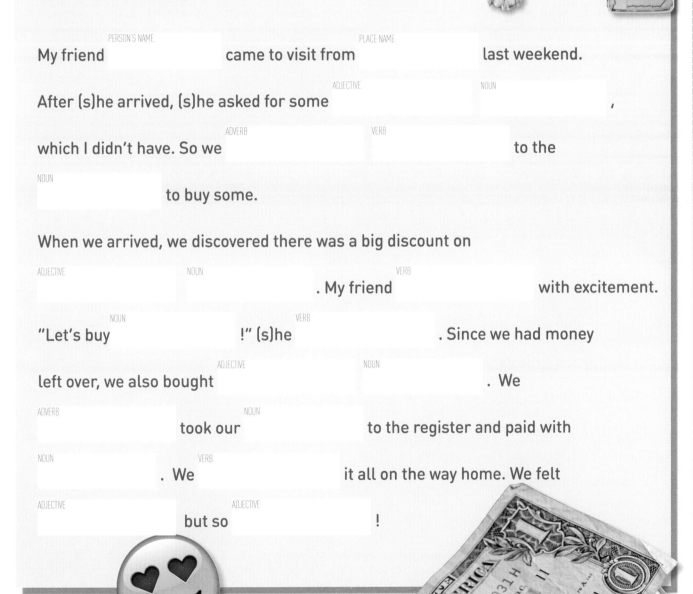

LIMERICK LINES

A LIMERICK IS A FUNNY, FIVE-LINE POEM that contains two sets of rhymes. The first, second, and fifth lines rhyme with one another, and the third and fourth lines rhyme with each other.

LINE 1: Tells us who the limerick is about
LINE 2: Tells us an extra detail about the person in Line 1
LINE 3: This shorter line tells us about something that happened to the person
LINE 4: This shorter line continues the thought from Line 3
LINE 5: This concluding line usually works like the punchline to a joke
(and sometimes ends with the same word as the first line)

For example, here are two limericks by Edward Lear, a Victorian poet who first popularized the limerick:

There was an old man with a beard,
Who said, "It is just as I feared!—
Two owls and a hen,
Four larks and a wren,
Have all built their nests in my beard!"

There was a young lady whose chin
Resembled the point of a pin;
So she had it made sharp,
And purchased a harp,
And played several tunes with her chin.

Write a limerick of your own by filling in the blanks below.

I once knew a _____ _____ with a _____ ,

Who thought every day was _____ _____ ,

But they didn't _____ _____ ,

And they _____ all the _____ ,

So they ended up _____ in _____ .

_____

STORY SETS

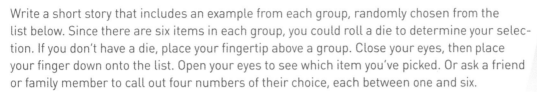

THERE ARE FOUR GROUPS OF WORDS IN THE LIST BELOW.

Each group covers a different aspect of the plot of a story.
The groups are:

• Location—where the story takes place
• Protagonist—who the story is about
• Event—something that takes place during the story
• Object—a physical item that is part of the story

Write a short story that includes an example from each group, randomly chosen from the list below. Since there are six items in each group, you could roll a die to determine your selection. If you don't have a die, place your fingertip above a group. Close your eyes, then place your finger down onto the list. Open your eyes to see which item you've picked. Or ask a friend or family member to call out four numbers of their choice, each between one and six.

LOCATION	PROTAGONIST	EVENT	OBJECT
1: A school	1: The king of England	1: A three-legged race	1: An alien spaceship
2: A swimming pool	2: A giant dog	2: A strange phone call	2: A pail of water
3: A zoo	3: A famous actor	3: An earthquake	3: A giant pizza
4: A space station	4: A medieval knight	4: An unexpected visitor	4: A polar bear
5: A shopping mall	5: A friendly dragon	5: A solar eclipse	5: A bag of footballs
6: A lost city	6: A clever cat	6: A very loud noise	6: A box of fireworks

Use the space below to write your story:

[BEHIND THE BRAIN]

If you sit down and try to write a story, you might find it tricky to get started. That's because there's an overwhelming number of possibilities! Methods like the one used in this puzzle—which narrow your choices significantly—are really helpful. Your brain likes to have guidance when starting a task. By taking prompts from the list, it is much easier to make the giant leap from a blank page to the first ideas for a story.

You can use this technique whenever you have trouble getting going on something. Look for a way to simplify the task, perhaps by finding an easy first step, or by reducing your options. You could even use a version of the method on this page. Write down some possible ideas, and then pick one at random.

LATERAL THINKING ANSWERS PAGE 150

IN "LATERAL THINKING" PUZZLES, YOU NEED TO COME UP WITH A CLEVER EXPLANATION FOR SOMETHING that otherwise seems impossible in some way.

Here's an example:

Q: Cowboy Dave rode into town on Tuesday, and left town five days later—also on Tuesday. How is this possible?

A: His **horse** is called Tuesday, so it can be true that he rode into town on Tuesday, and also rode out on Tuesday.

GIDDY UP TUESDAY!

PUZZLE 1
A window cleaner is standing on a ledge, cleaning the windows on the 10th floor of a building. Suddenly, there is a strong gust of wind, and he falls off the ledge. He is not attached to the building in any way, and falls freely until he reaches the ground but is not hurt at all. How is this possible?

PUZZLE 2
Usually, red means "stop now" and green means "go now." But can you think of a situation in which red means "go" and green means "stop"?

PUZZLE 3
What is lost whenever it is shared?

LOGICAL THINKING

ANSWERS PAGE 150

NOT ALL TRICKY PUZZLES INVOLVE TRICKS. Some of them just require you to think carefully—to use logic. Try the logic-based puzzles on this page. There's no hidden cleverness this time; they are all examples of puzzles that many people tend to get wrong.

PUZZLE 1

A red toy and a blue toy cost $1.10 in total. The blue toy costs $1 more than the red toy. How much does the red toy cost?

THINK CAREFULLY: Most people think that the answer is 10¢—but they're wrong!

PUZZLE 2

You have four double-sided cards. One side has a letter on it, and one side has a number on it. You can see one side of each of the cards below.

A friend states that every card with a vowel on one side has an even number on the other side. Which cards would you need to turn over to prove whether your friend is correct?

PUZZLE 3

Princess Peach is looking just at Dozy Dave. Dozy Dave, in turn, is looking just at Barky Bill. Princess Peach is a dog, and Barky Bill is a cat. Dozy Dave is either a dog or a cat, but you don't know which.
Given this information, is a dog looking at a cat? Or do you not know for sure?

DOTTY ART

THE PICTURE ON THIS PAGE MIGHT LOOK LIKE IT IS JUST A BUNCH OF DOTS, but that's because you haven't worked your creative magic yet!

Grab a pen or pencil, and start drawing lines to join pairs of dots in whatever way you like. Once you have drawn five or six lines, take a step back and see if the image has started to remind you of something: A bird? A building? An animal? If so, then start joining dots that you think will help make it look even more like that object. Or, if not, add a few more lines and then check again. Even if you never recognize anything in the lines, you'll still end up with a cool, creative pattern.

[BEHIND THE BRAIN]

When you joined the dots, did you start to see a picture of something you recognized? Our brains have an incredible power to recognize images, even when we have only a limited view of them. It's why, for thousands of years, humanity has looked up to the stars—tiny white dots in the sky—and joined them together to form all manner of creatures. We call them constellations.

In truth, only the area right in front of us is in sharp focus. Most of the rest of our field of vision is actually quite fuzzy and blurred. We need to turn our heads or move our eyes to get a clear view of other areas. Our brains are, therefore, used to working on very limited information when working out what we're looking at. So, when viewing the dots—or stars—we are quite capable of "seeing" things that aren't really there.

SOME ASSEMBLY REQUIRED ANSWERS PAGE 151

TRACE THIS SET OF SHAPES ONTO A PIECE OF PAPER. Cut out each shape along its borders to make seven separate pieces. (You don't need to color the shapes, but you can if you want.)

Now, try to rearrange your pieces to make each of the following pictures. This kind of puzzle is called a tangram.

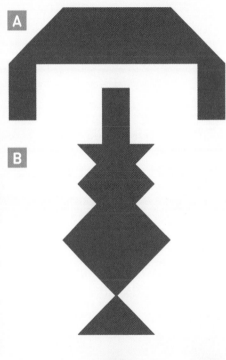

COLORED RECTANGLES

FOR THIS CREATIVE CHALLENGE, PICK FOUR COLORED PENS, PENCILS, OR CRAYONS.
Start by choosing your favorite color. Add three more colors that you think all go with your favorite color. Then color the picture as you please, using one color per rectangle.

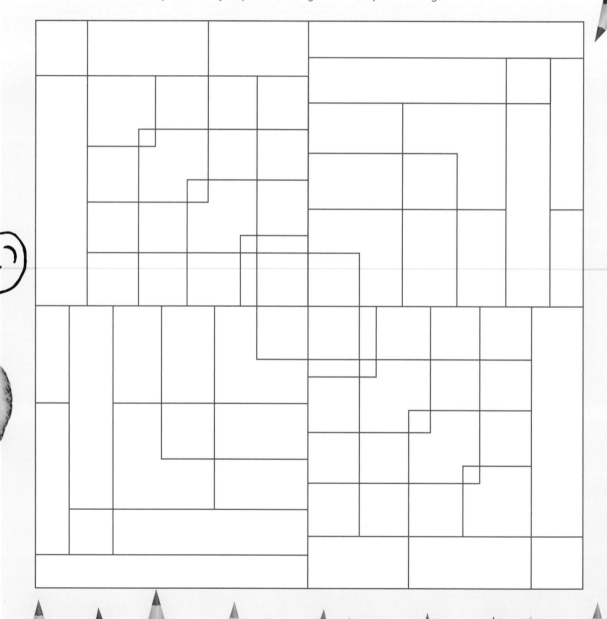

CIRCULAR CHALLENGE

NOW, COLOR IN THIS PICTURE USING YOUR FOUR COLORS. See if you can avoid having two touching areas that are filled with the same color.

It's possible to color this image using just two colors that don't touch. Without coloring it, can you figure out how you can do this? ANSWER PAGE 151

SLIDING BLOCK PUZZLE

COPY THESE SHAPES ONTO A PIECE OF HEAVY PAPER OR CARDBOARD, then cut them out. Color them in the same way shown.

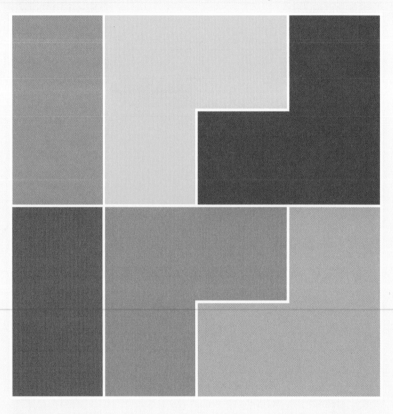

PUZZLE 1

You're now going to use the empty grid on the opposite page to form a playing board. Place the pieces you've made onto the board, so they are laid out in this arrangement:

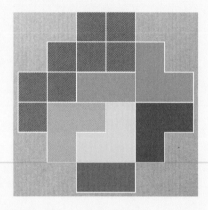

Now, move the pieces around so that you can slide the red rectangle from its starting point to out of the opening at the top of the board. You are allowed to slide any piece either horizontally or vertically, but not diagonally. A piece must always finish each move with its edges against the white grid lines. Also, when you slide a piece, it can't move over or onto another piece at any point, or over any of the solid walls.

You'll need to move all the other pieces around as you try to move the red piece to the "exit." It might take you a while, but it is possible!

PUZZLE 2

This puzzle grid is trickier, but the goal is the same: slide the red piece out of the grid.

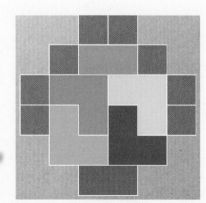

EXIT

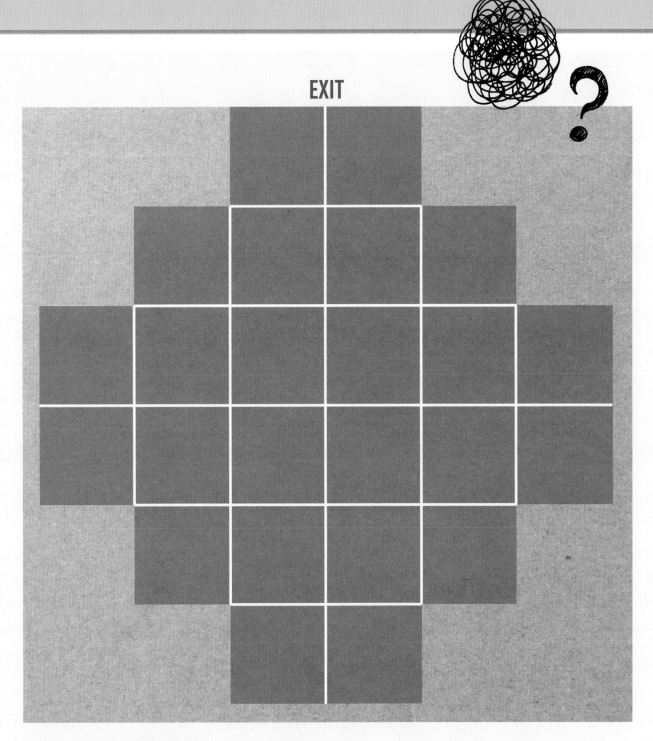

PUZZLES 3 AND 4

For a bonus challenge, set up the grid as you did for Puzzle 1 or for Puzzle 2. Now, see if you can slide the blue piece out of the grid. It's much trickier than the red piece, but it's possible for both puzzles.

TIME TRIALS

CIRCLE LINK <small>ANSWER PAGE 151</small>

Draw horizontal and vertical lines to join the circles into pairs, so that each pair contains one yellow circle and one blue circle. Lines can't cross each other, and they also can't cross over another circle. Every circle must be part of exactly **one** pair.

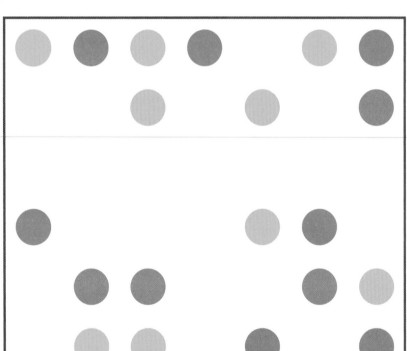

TIME STARTED	TIME ENDED	TOTAL TIME

NUMBER DARTS ANSWER PAGE 151

Add together one number from the outer ring, one from the middle ring, and one from the inner ring so that their sum equals the first total below. Repeat the process so that your sums match the second, then the third total. For example, you could form a total of 12 by adding 5 from the inner ring, 3 from the middle ring, and 4 from the outer ring.

Totals: 22 25 28

TIME STARTED	TIME ENDED	TOTAL TIME
:	:	:

CHAPTER SIX
COMMUNICATION

Humans are constantly communicating—whether we realize it or not. Of course, we use words to explain our feelings and to get across our ideas. But we also communicate with the tone of our voice, our facial expressions, our body posture—even the music we listen to.

Communication is so important for human beings that our brains have specific areas devoted to analyzing and interpreting speech, controlling how we talk, processing body language, and keeping track of faces. Our complex communication is one thing that makes humans different from other animals. Want to test your skills? Learn about cutting-edge communication research, then see if you can solve these puzzles. →

SHOUT OUT

WORD **ORBIT**

ANSWER PAGE 151

HOW MANY WORDS CAN YOU MAKE FROM THESE ORBITING LETTERS? Choose one letter from the outer ring, one letter from the middle ring, and one letter from the inner ring to spell out each word.

For example, you might pick M from the outer ring, A from the middle ring, and N from the inner ring to spell MAN.

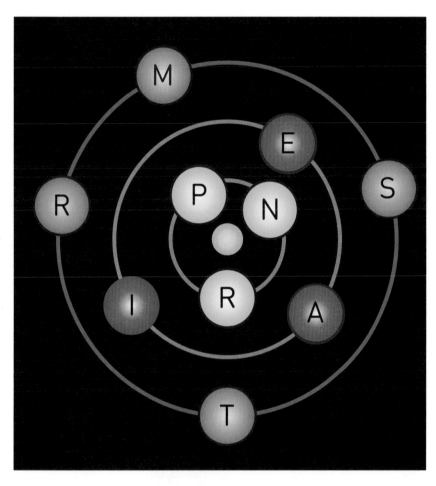

SCORE RANGES

5 WORDS = GOOD
10 WORDS = EXCELLENT
15 WORDS = AMAZING

connect

NEURAL NETWORKING

SPEAK YOUR MIND! THE HUMAN BRAIN IS WIRED TO CONNECT WITH OTHERS. HERE ARE SOME OF BRAIN SCIENCE'S MOST ASTOUNDING EXPERIMENTS ON COMMUNICATION.

FACE IT

Do you never forget a face? Or do you struggle to recall what your kindergarten teacher looked like? While some people are better than others at recalling faces, all humans seem to have a natural ability to keep track of what people look like. But how many faces can we actually know? That's the question researchers set out to answer in 2018.

The researchers asked participants to complete different exercises that tested their knowledge of faces, like writing down as many faces as they knew from their personal lives, as well as famous faces like actors and politicians. They also showed the participants thousands of photos of famous people and asked which ones they recognized.

The results showed that people have a truly astounding ability to remember faces: Most could recall around 5,000, and some up to 10,000! It makes sense that people are good at this skill. The ability to recall faces is important, allowing us to keep track of our social relationships. How many faces do you think you know?

A FAST-FOOD **RESTAURANT** IN CHINA USES **FACIAL RECOGNITION TECHNOLOGY** TO ALLOW PEOPLE TO PAY FOR THEIR MEAL BY **SMILING** AT THE CAMERA.

COLORFUL LANGUAGE

Could the language you speak change the way you think? It's a question that neuroscientists have been fascinated with for a long time. One of the latest studies on the question, in 2018, analyzed how people who speak different languages perceive color.

In German—as in English—there is one word for the color blue. But in Greek and Russian, there are separate words for "light blue" and "dark blue." Scientists were curious whether this language difference could change how the speakers see color. So while they scanned the brains of volunteers who spoke German, Greek, and Russian, they showed them a series of pictures of colored triangles on a colored background. Sometimes, a light blue triangle would appear on top of a slightly darker blue background. Other times, it was a light green triangle on top of a slightly darker green background. Then they asked the volunteers whether they had been able to spot the triangle.

The German speakers (who only have one word for blue, as well as one word for green) did not show a

difference in their ability to spot the triangle whether it was blue or green. But the Greek and Russian speakers (who have separate words for light blue and dark blue, but only one word for green) were better at spotting the light blue triangle placed against a darker blue background than they were at spotting the light green triangle placed against a darker green background.

Researchers think that the separate words for light blue and dark blue in Greek and Russian may make speakers of these languages more aware of slight differences between shades of blue—and therefore make them better able to spot the light blue triangle. But because they don't have separate words for different shades of green, they were no better at spotting the light green triangle than the German speakers. While you wouldn't think that the words you use could actually change the way you see the world, this study shows that, in fact, they just might!

SPEAKING WITH SONG

From a classical orchestra to a simple drumbeat, music takes all kinds of forms. In fact, nearly every culture on Earth has its own music. And now, scientists think that even though music is very different from place to place, certain traits are shared by all music everywhere, making music a kind of "universal language."

Researchers asked 750 people from 60 countries to listen to short clips of songs from around the globe. Then they asked the participants to judge whether the song was for dancing, for soothing a baby, telling a story, mourning the dead, and so on. Most of the listeners, even though they were unfamiliar with the music, were able to tell right away what the song was for. Interestingly, the only type of song people had trouble identifying was love songs. Hey, love can be confusing!

OPPOSITES ANSWERS PAGE 151

CAN YOU DRAW LINES TO JOIN THESE WORDS INTO PAIRS OF OPPOSITES? Think before your draw: Some words mean the opposite of more than one word, but each word can be used only in one pair. That means there's only one way to pair all the words.

dark stop black start

slow

white dangerous night difficult

innocent safe

finish go

first last

day forget

cowardly brave soft

light remember

fast past

hard

future guilty easy

PREFIXES AND SUFFIXES ANSWERS PAGE 151

EACH OF THESE WORDS CAN HAVE EITHER A PREFIX OR SUFFIX from the lists below attached to it to make a new word. A **prefix** attaches to the beginning of a word, and a **suffix** attaches to the end of a word. Write down the new words, using all the words, prefixes, and suffixes one time.

WORDS		PREFIXES	SUFFIXES
AFFORD	BIOGRAPHY	AUTO	ABLE
CIRCLE	COOK	EXTRA	DOM
FORGIVE	KING	INTER	LESS
LEADER	NATIONAL	OVER	NESS
ORDINARY	THOUGHT	SEMI	SHIP

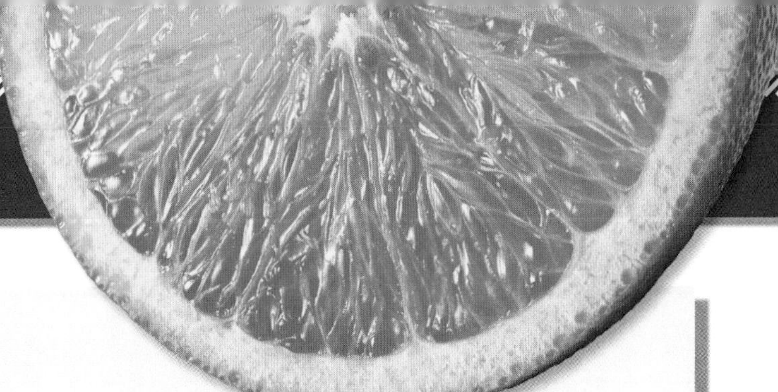

SETS

ANSWERS PAGE 151

PLACE EACH OF THE FOLLOWING WORDS INTO ONE OF THE FOUR SETS BELOW, so that each word is used once and each set contains exactly four items. Be careful: Some of the words could fit in more than one set. However, there is only one way of placing four words in each set without reusing any words.

WORDS

BLUE	DIAMOND	LEMON	SAPPHIRE
BRONZE	EMERALD	ORANGE	SILVER
BROWN	GOLD	PINEAPPLE	TIN
CHERRY	LAVENDER	RUBY	YELLOW

COLORS   FRUIT   METALS   PRECIOUS STONES

ANAGRAMS ANSWERS PAGE 151

AN ANAGRAM IS A WORD THAT HAS HAD ITS LETTERS REARRANGED. For example, ADGORN is an anagram of DRAGON.

All of the following are anagrams of colors. Solve each anagram to reveal the original color.

1. DER   ANSWER →

2. BELU   ANSWER →

3. IKNP   ANSWER →

4. EEGNR   ANSWER →

5. EHITW   ANSWER →

6. ELPPRU   ANSWER →

Can you also solve the following anagrams to reveal six types of fruit?

1. UMPL   ANSWER →

2. NABAAN   ANSWER →

3. BREELRUBY   ANSWER →

4. WIKI   ANSWER →

5. TRINECANE   ANSWER →

6. LAWENOMERT   ANSWER →

ANAGRAM SENTENCES

ANSWERS PAGE 151

IN EACH OF THE FOLLOWING SENTENCES, ONE WORD IS MISSING. Can you find an anagram of the CAPITALIZED word in each sentence that can fill the blank spot? One sentence is completed for you as an example.

1. She squirted **LEMON** juice onto the __MELON__ to keep it fresh.

2. She saw the _____ jump up, then **ACT** very strangely.

3. His leg **ACHES**, every time they _____ the dog.

4. When she stopped to **LISTEN**, she noticed that it was completely _____ .

5. When he went into his **STUDY**, he noticed his desk was very _____ .

6. The **UNWARY** bird wandered onto the _____ .

7. The _____ left **STREAKS** on the ice.

8. When he was **STRESSED**, he sometimes ate too many _____ .

[BEHIND THE BRAIN]

Did you find some of these easier than others—but you didn't know why? It all comes down to how you see the anagram first. Your brain forms some initial ideas about the letters as soon as you look at them, and then it's very hard to see them differently. To avoid this effect, try writing out the letters in a different way. You could make your own anagram, putting the letters in a different order. Or write them in a circle. This way, the letters aren't connected like in a word, and your brain is less likely to make unhelpful assumptions. And if that *still* doesn't work, try writing them in a chaotic jumble, as if they're floating about in the sky. It can really help!

WORD LADDERS

ANSWERS PAGE 151

FOR EACH OF THESE WORD LADDERS, CONVERT THE TOP WORD INTO THE BOTTOM WORD. At each step you can change only one letter, and you can't rearrange the order of the letters.

To help you solve the puzzles, we've given you clues, as well an example.

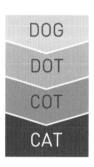

DOG
DOT
COT
CAT

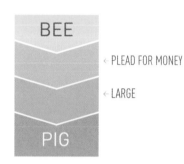

BEE
← PLEAD FOR MONEY
← LARGE
PIG

COW
← POLICEMAN
← BURST
← BABY DOG
PUG

WORD PYRAMID

ANSWER PAGE 151

USE THE CLUES TO FILL IN THIS WORD PYRAMID. Each row contains the same letters as the row above, plus one extra, although the letters might be arranged in a different order.

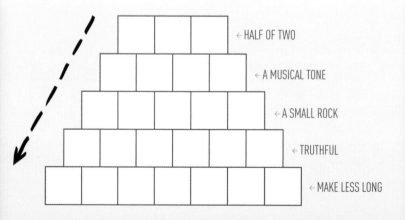

← HALF OF TWO

← A MUSICAL TONE

← A SMALL ROCK

← TRUTHFUL

← MAKE LESS LONG

WORD STACKS

ANSWERS PAGE 151

IN EACH PUZZLE, a single three-letter word has been deleted from all four words in the set. Figure out what that three-letter word is, and then write it in the blank spaces to reveal the four original words in the set.

PUZZLE 1

B [ ][ ][ ] E S T

[ ][ ][ ] R E S S

P [ ][ ][ ] L I N G

S [ ][ ][ ] L E

PUZZLE 2

C [ ][ ][ ] I T S

I N G [ ][ ][ ] I E N T

P [ ][ ][ ] I C T

T I [ ][ ][ ] N E S S

LINK WORDS

ANSWERS PAGE 151

A "LINK WORD" IS A WORD THAT CAN BE ADDED TO THE END OF THE FIRST WORD IN A PAIR, AS WELL AS THE START OF THE SECOND WORD TO MAKE TWO ENTIRELY NEW WORDS.

For example, WORK _ _ _ GROW could be solved by inserting the word "OUT," since this would make WORKOUT and OUTGROW.

Find a "link word" to connect each pair of words in this set.

1 B A R E [ ][ ][ ] B A L L

2 D A Y [ ][ ][ ] H O U S E

3 S U P E R [ ][ ][ ] F I S H

PHRASE FINDER ANSWER PAGE 152

Place the letters in each column into one of the unshaded boxes immediately beneath to form the words of a hidden sentence. The letters aren't necessarily shown in the correct order within each column, so you'll need to figure out how far down to place each letter. The shaded boxes represent spaces between words. The quotation will read from left to right along each row, working from top to bottom.

YES

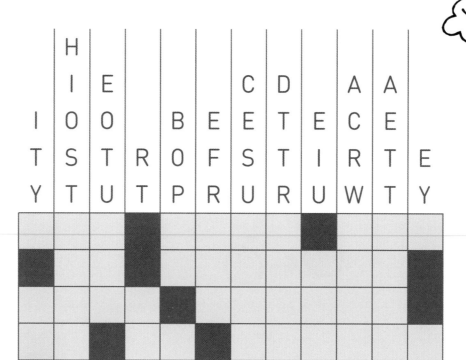

[BEHIND THE BRAIN]

At the beginning of this puzzle, the letters were all jumbled up, which made the words nearly impossible to read. Sometimes, though, you actually can read certain jumbled words with relative ease.

For example, try reading this sentence with the letters jumbled in each word: "No Adonmy I entw ot eht akrp". Now try this version instead: "On Mdnoay I wnte to teh pkar."

Even though the letters are still mixed up, the first letter of each word was correct. Your brain remembers words based on their first letter. (Picture a great big filing cabinet that has one drawer for words that start with A, another for B, and so on.) This made the second version of the sentence much easier to unscramble into its correct form: "On Monday I went to the park."

INTERPRETATION REQUIRED

ANSWERS PAGE 152

SOME WELL-KNOWN EXPRESSIONS HAVE BEEN CHANGED so that different words are being used to describe the same idea. For example, "a dime a dozen" might be changed to "a 10-cent coin every 12 items." Can you decipher the original expression? If you get stuck, a clue for each is given at the bottom of the page.

1. A slice of a crumbly dessert
ANSWER →

2. Look at the text that's written under one row of letters and above the next
ANSWER →

3. Failed to catch the ship
ANSWER →

4. Change an extended tale into a briefer one
ANSWER →

5. Felines and canines are falling from the clouds
ANSWER →

6. Preferable to arrive after the deadline than not at all
ANSWER →

CLUES: 1. EASY 2. LOOK FOR THE UNDERLYING MESSAGE 3. ARRIVE TOO LATE 4. GET TO THE POINT 5. BAD WEATHER 6. DOING SOMETHING BEHIND SCHEDULE IS BETTER THAN NOT DOING IT

PICTURE PHRASES

ANSWERS PAGE 152

CAN YOU WORK OUT WHICH well-known expression is represented by each of these two picture clues?

1

ANSWER →

2

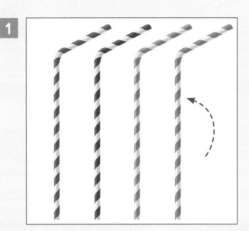

ANSWER →

WORD FIT ANSWERS PAGE 152

Place all of the listed words into the grid, either horizontally or vertically, with one letter per box.

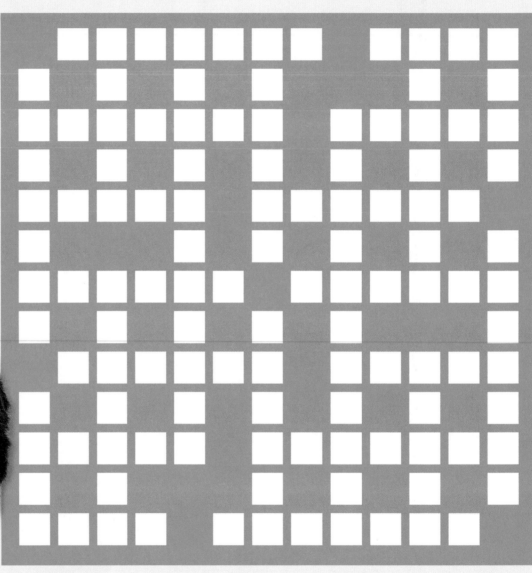

4 LETTERS	5 LETTERS	6 LETTERS	7 LETTERS	11 LETTERS
EURO	AFTER	ADVENT	ACTRESS	ARRANGEMENT
EYES	AURAL	ANCHOR	CARAVAN	ENVIRONMENT
LOVE	CABLE	EARWIG	OSTRICH	
SIDE	EXCEL	SPRING	PARENTS	
	RULER	STATUE	REDUCED	
	YACHT	TINSEL	TREMBLE	
			TROLLEY	
			WEATHER	

WORD GRID SEARCH

ANSWER PAGE 152

CAN YOU FIND THE WORD "BRAIN" SOMEWHERE in this web of letters? Start on any letter B and then follow lines to neighboring letters until you have successfully spelled out the word.

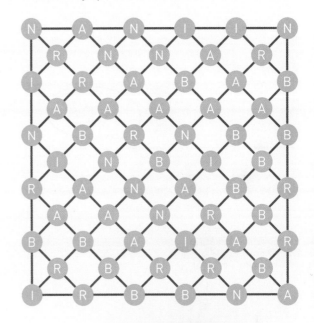

WORD PATH SEARCH

ANSWERS PAGE 152

THIS PUZZLE CONTAINS 10 HIDDEN COUNTRY NAMES. To find them, trace a continuous path that visits every letter only once, moving left/right/up/down between letters to spell out the countries. (You cannot move diagonally.) The first country on the path, Mexico, is highlighted in the puzzle to show you how it works. Now extend the path up to the F, and continue drawing it until you have spelled out nine more countries.

```
A N A I R I I N
R C P N B T A A
F E S A R T S U
O C I L H I N A
M E X I C Y N I
L A G A R M A N
R T U G E A C D
O P A D A N A I
```

SINGLE-WORD WORD SEARCH

ANSWER PAGE 152

CAN YOU FIND THE WORD "GAMES" IN THIS WORD SEARCH? It is hidden only once, but it might be written in any direction and could face either forward or backward.

HI!

```
M E G E G M G A S A
E S E S A A S E M E
M E G A E S S M S A
E E E A S G M E M A
M M E E S E M E M S
G S E S M A M E S M
S G A M E M M A E G
G A E S E M M G G G
S S G E G A G A S M
S A M M A S S A G S
```

WRAPAROUND WORD SEARCH

ANSWERS PAGE 152

Can you find the following names of nocturnal animals in this word search? They can be written in any direction, including diagonally—**and** they can "wrap around" from one side of the puzzle to the other. (Imagine that the puzzle continues in all directions beyond the grid.)

One word is already highlighted to show how it works. Notice how HYENA starts on the H at the bottom of the puzzle, then wraps around to the top of the next column of the puzzle.

```
U O P K S O Y U N O
N R U W M O S E C C
U N O O C H P C N C
K H W M I A O O H A
P L S S P M O C N R
U C R O P S E N I P
N U T O N T P O O C
M M O U S E M O A R
A O U O O R U A E N
S N S S S H O T R O
```

WORDS
HAMSTER
~~HYENA~~
MOUSE
OPOSSUM
OWL
PORCUPINE
RACCOON
SKUNK

MISSING MIDDLE WORD SEARCH ANSWERS PAGE 152

FIND EACH OF THESE MOUNTAINS IN THE WORD SEARCH GRID. However, there's a challenge: Some of the letters are missing from the grid. It's up to you to write them in. Figure out which letter to place into each of the 16 empty squares (marked by dashed lines), so that all 14 mountain names can be found in the puzzle.

A	B	P	R	N	E	O	R	V	O	A	N	E	N
G	C	E	O	L	O	G	A	N	U	O	E	E	L
N	C	A	N	P	L	C	S	G	O	N	K	A	H
U	O	Y	M	N	O	J	A	Y	Á	H	R	H	O
J	O	E	E	I	E	C	R	R	A	K	U	S	T
N	Z	A	S	L					B	N	E	R	S
E	A	A	U	O					I	V	G	L	E
H	R	N	C	L					E	N	A	S	O
C	O	A	S	A					L	P	I	N	R
G	B	N	U	A	B	K	E	E	N	U	E	A	O
N	M	H	E	R	N	S	A	R	D	J	J	T	R
A	I	O	U	Z	T	E	V	M	H	V	I	C	L
K	H	S	E	L	I	B	E	A	U	A	A	H	Z
E	C	O	R	A	J	N	A	M	I	L	I	K	N

MOUNTAINS
ACONCAGUA
BEN NEVIS
CHIMBORAZO
DENALI
ELBRUS
EVEREST
HUASCARÁN
KANGCHENJUNGA
KILIMANJARO
LHOTSE
LOGAN
MAKALU
POPOCATEPETL
RAINIER

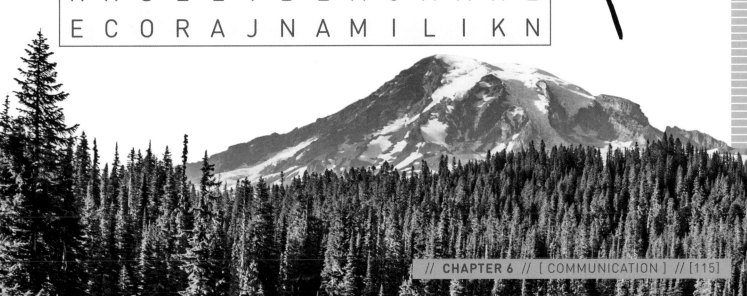

WORDS WITHIN WORDS   ANSWERS PAGE 152

EACH OF THE FOLLOWING SENTENCES CONTAINS A HIDDEN COLOR, formed by removing the spaces and punctuation between two or more words and reading across sequential letters. The first one is done for you as an example.

1. The cab lacked doors.   (HIDDEN COLOR: BLACK)

2. My eyebrow nearly got removed.

3. She used to yell, owing to her bad knee.

4. The ogre endangered them all.

5. The railway spur pleased the town.

6. You can go to the bakery for angelic, delicious desserts!

7. The cow hit every fence as it tried to escape.

8. This car let her drive more easily.

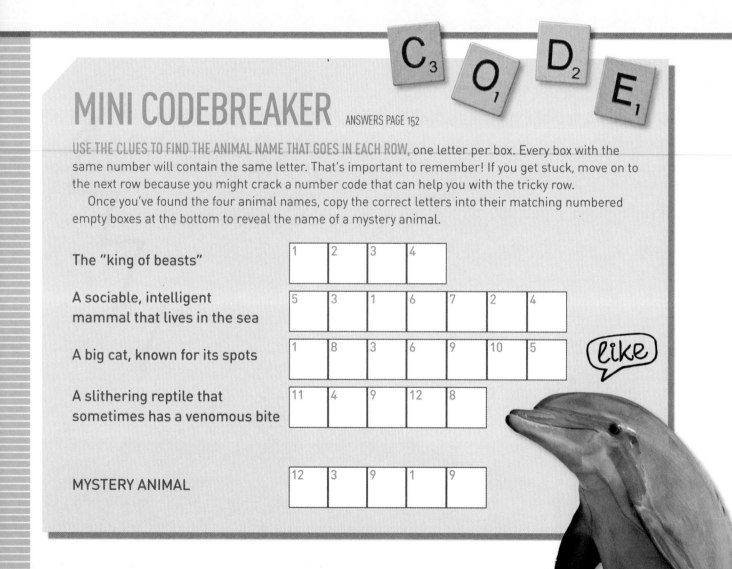

MINI CODEBREAKER   ANSWERS PAGE 152

USE THE CLUES TO FIND THE ANIMAL NAME THAT GOES IN EACH ROW, one letter per box. Every box with the same number will contain the same letter. That's important to remember! If you get stuck, move on to the next row because you might crack a number code that can help you with the tricky row.

   Once you've found the four animal names, copy the correct letters into their matching numbered empty boxes at the bottom to reveal the name of a mystery animal.

The "king of beasts"
1	2	3	4

A sociable, intelligent mammal that lives in the sea
5	3	1	6	7	2	4

A big cat, known for its spots
1	8	3	6	9	10	5

like

A slithering reptile that sometimes has a venomous bite
11	4	9	12	8

MYSTERY ANIMAL
12	3	9	1	9

INITIAL SEQUENCES

ANSWERS PAGE 152

CAN YOU IDENTIFY EACH OF THE FOLLOWING SEQUENCES, GIVEN JUST THE FIRST TWO LETTERS OF EACH WORD? For example, "Mo Tu We Th Fr" would be Monday, Tuesday, Wednesday, Thursday, Friday: the days of the week in order.

1 | On | Tw | Th | Fo | Fi | Si | Se | ANSWER →

2 | Me | Ve | Ea | Ma | Ju | Sa | Ur | ANSWER →

3 | Re | Or | Ye | Gr | Bl | In | Vi | ANSWER →

4 | Fi | Se | Th | Fo | Fi | Si | Se | ANSWER →

CODEBREAKER

ANSWER PAGE 153

Change each letter in the text below to the one immediately **before** it in the alphabet to reveal a hidden message.

Dpohsbuvmbujpot po sfwfbmjoh uif tfdsfu ufyu.

ANSWER →

WORD CIRCLE
ANSWERS PAGE 153

HOW MANY WORDS CAN YOU FIND IN THIS WORD CIRCLE? Each word must use the center letter plus two or more of the other letters. There is one word that uses every letter.

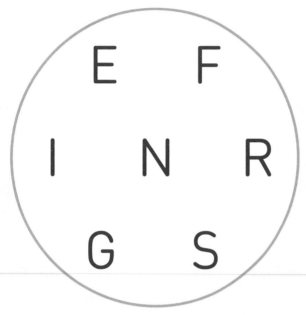

SCORE RANGES

10 WORDS = GOOD
20 WORDS = EXCELLENT
30 WORDS = AMAZING

WORD SQUARE

ANSWERS PAGE 153

FIND WORDS IN THIS WORD SQUARE BY STARTING ON ANY LETTER and then tracing a path to touching letters. Move up, down, left, right, or diagonally between squares. Each word must have three or more letters. You can visit a square only once within a single word. There is one word that uses every square.

SCORE RANGES

8 WORDS = GOOD
15 WORDS = EXCELLENT
20 WORDS = AMAZING

WORD SLIDER

ANSWERS PAGE 153

How many words can you form in the purple box by "sliding" each column of letters up and down? One word is already made for you as an example.

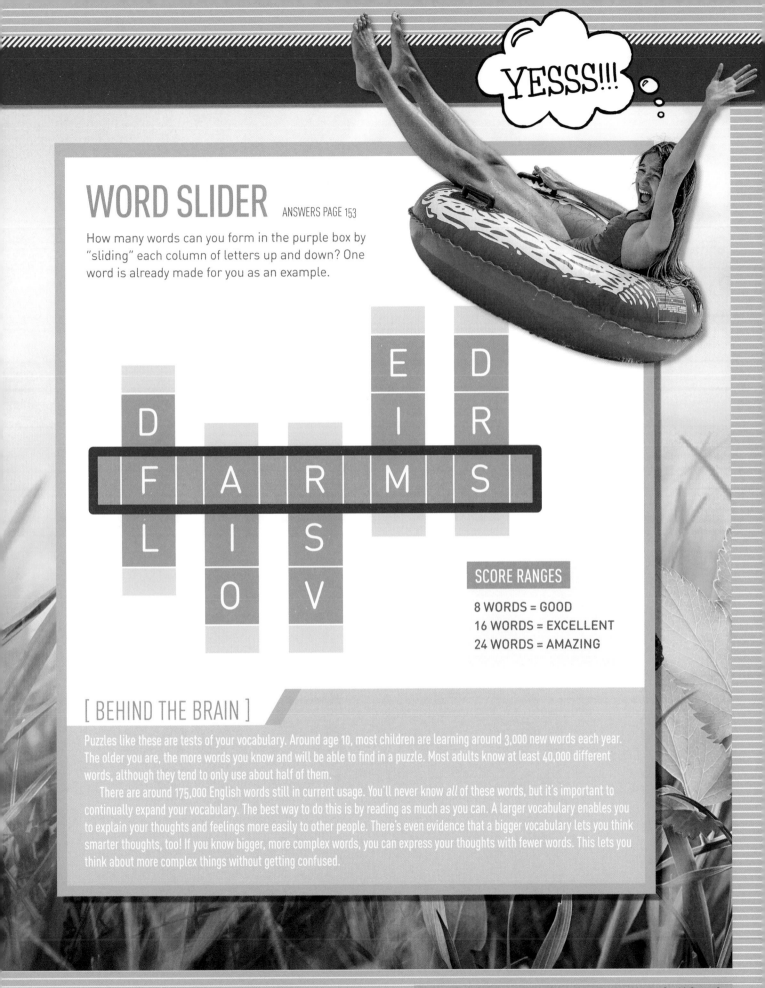

SCORE RANGES

8 WORDS = GOOD
16 WORDS = EXCELLENT
24 WORDS = AMAZING

[BEHIND THE BRAIN]

Puzzles like these are tests of your vocabulary. Around age 10, most children are learning around 3,000 new words each year. The older you are, the more words you know and will be able to find in a puzzle. Most adults know at least 40,000 different words, although they tend to only use about half of them.

There are around 175,000 English words still in current usage. You'll never know *all* of these words, but it's important to continually expand your vocabulary. The best way to do this is by reading as much as you can. A larger vocabulary enables you to explain your thoughts and feelings more easily to other people. There's even evidence that a bigger vocabulary lets you think smarter thoughts, too! If you know bigger, more complex words, you can express your thoughts with fewer words. This lets you think about more complex things without getting confused.

CIRCLE LINK ANSWER PAGE 153

Draw horizontal and vertical lines to join the circles into pairs, so that each pair contains one teal circle and one green circle. Lines can't cross each other, and they also can't cross over another circle. Every circle must be part of exactly **one** pair.

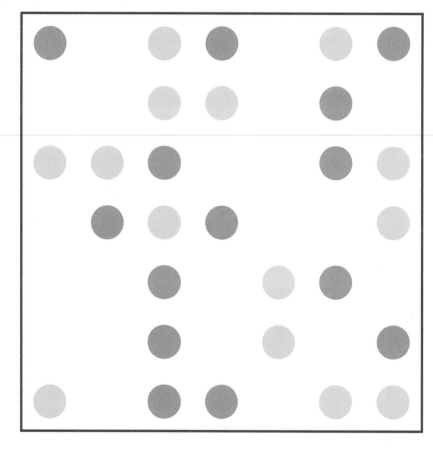

TIME STARTED

TIME ENDED

TOTAL TIME

→ You've become a super solver! How fast can you ace these puzzles in this round? Grab a pencil and timer as you tackle these two familiar puzzles.

NUMBER DARTS ANSWER PAGE 153

Add together one number from the outer ring, one from the middle ring, and one from the inner ring so that their sum equals the first total below. Repeat the process so that your sums match the second, then the third total. For example, you could form a total of 11 by adding 6 from the inner ring, 3 from the middle ring, and 2 from the outer ring.

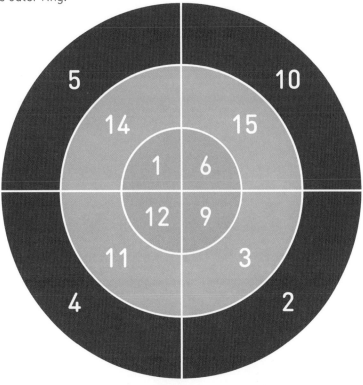

Totals: 18 23 32

TIME STARTED

TIME ENDED

TOTAL TIME

CHAPTER **SEVEN**

HACKING THE BRAIN

You know that the brain can keep changing and growing as you learn. The puzzles in this book have challenged your cranium, exercised your mental muscles, and maybe even bulked up your brain. But are there other ways you can boost your brainpower?

As brain science grows more sophisticated, experts are discovering ways to train the brain to keep it functioning better longer, help people retain new information, and perhaps even share information instantly. See for yourself, then put your brain-building to the test with the most mind-bending puzzles yet. Are you up for the cranial challenge?

$\longrightarrow$

STRAW **PUZZLE**

ANSWER PAGE 153

GET READY TO REV UP YOUR BRAIN—YOU'LL NEED SOME EXTRA-SMART THINKING to figure out how to start and solve the tricky puzzles in this chapter.

Imagine that you have 12 straws laid out as follows, forming 3 squares. Can you move exactly 3 straws, so that you end up with 5 squares?

BRAIN BOOST

WILL IT SOMEDAY BE POSSIBLE TO HACK THE BRAIN TO HELP YOU REMEMBER MORE, LEARN WITH LESS EFFORT—OR EVEN SEND THOUGHTS FROM ONE BRAIN TO ANOTHER? READ ON AND DECIDE FOR YOURSELF!

MENTAL WORKOUT

Everyone knows that exercise is good for your body. But did you know it's good for your brain, too? Many studies have suggested that staying active throughout life lowers the risk of memory problems as people age. In 2014, researchers found that it might have this effect by increasing the size of the hippocampus, the area of the brain involved in memory and learning.

Participants in the 2014 study experienced this effect when they walked at a brisk pace for one hour, twice a week. But scientists think anything that gets your heart pumping should work, including swimming, tennis, dancing, or even vacuuming or raking leaves. So if you want to give your brain a boost, get moving!

UNFORGETTABLE FONT

Have you ever read something only to have the information disappear from your brain as soon as you've finished? Scientists think it may be possible to help people remember what they've read—simply by changing the font.

A group of researchers set out to create the new font in 2018. Their idea was based on a theory that says people may remember things better when their brains have to make extra effort to process the information. The font they created, named Sans Forgetica, depicts letters with sections removed, and tilts them backward. Reading it requires extra focus and attention. The experiment is still in an early stage, but so far, testing suggests that reading information in the new font makes a small but significant difference in peoples' ability to remember: While participants remembered 50 percent of what they'd read in standard Arial font, they recalled 57 percent of what they'd read in Sans Forgetica. Someday, this research could help experts design books or websites in ways that give the brain a memory boost.

ARE YOU THINKING WHAT I'M THINKING?

Sending your thoughts to another person's brain is the stuff of science fiction—isn't it? In 2015, researchers connected the brains of two humans. In one laboratory, a professor sat wearing a cap that measured electrical activity in his brain. In another lab across campus, another professor sat wearing a purple swim cap that could send a magnetic impulse to the part of his brain that controlled the movement of his finger.

Then the first professor played a video game with his mind. When he was supposed to fire a cannon at an invading space alien on the screen, he would imagine moving his finger to hit the "fire" button. Across campus, the other professor couldn't see or hear the game. But without him trying, his finger would move at just the right moment and hit the button.

With their connected brains, the two professors sitting in different rooms across campus were able to use their combined mental power to successfully play a game. Scientists say that they're nowhere near being able to send complex thoughts between two brains—but they're just getting started.

TOUCHY

ANSWER PAGE 153

PLACE A NUMBER FROM 1 TO 6 into each empty square, so that no number repeats in any row or column. Identical numbers cannot touch, not even diagonally.

	3			4	
		5	1		
3					1
4					6
		4	5		
	1			6	

SAMPLE PUZZLE

4	1	3	2	6	5
5	2	6	1	3	4
6	3	4	5	2	1
2	5	1	6	4	3
1	4	2	3	5	6
3	6	5	4	1	2

TRIO SUDOKU

ANSWER PAGE 153

PLACE A NUMBER FROM 1 TO 6 into each empty square, so that no number repeats in any row, column, or bold-lined 3x2 box. Any completely empty square can have only a 1 or 2 placed into it. A square containing a smaller square must contain either a 3 or 4. And a square with a circle must contain either a 5 or 6.

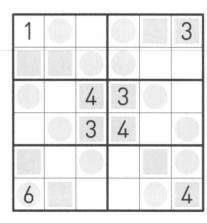

SAMPLE PUZZLE

2	5	1	6	3	4
4	6	3	2	1	5
1	2	4	5	6	3
6	3	5	1	4	2
3	1	2	4	5	6
5	4	6	3	2	1

[BEHIND THE BRAIN]

When you solved these puzzles, you probably had to count "1, 2, 3, 4, 5, 6" in your head in order to work out which numbers were missing. The secret to solving these puzzles quickly, however, is to keep practicing until you don't have to count. The fastest sudoku solvers can simply glance at a row, column, or box and see immediately which numbers are missing without having to consciously think about it. Their brains have become so good at spotting possible number patterns that they can immediately tell which parts are missing without any conscious thought.

Just how fast are the fastest? The world record was set in 2018 by Shiyao Wang of China. He solved a full-size sudoku—which has 81 squares, containing numbers from 1 to 9— in an astonishing 54 seconds!

JIGSAW SUDOKU

ANSWER PAGE 153

PLACE A NUMBER FROM 1 TO 6 into each empty square, so that no number repeats in any row, column, or bold-lined region.

			4	2	
4		2			5
5			2		6
	3	4			

SAMPLE PUZZLE

5	2	6	3	1	4
2	3	4	1	6	5
6	1	3	5	4	2
3	4	1	2	5	6
1	6	5	4	2	3
4	5	2	6	3	1

BLACKOUT SUDOKU   ANSWER PAGE 153

PLACE A NUMBER FROM 1 TO 6 into each empty square, so that no number repeats in any row, column, or bold-lined 3x2 region. Do not write a number in the blacked-out square in each bold-lined region.

If you are used to regular sudoku, take care: The blacked-out square doesn't always represent the same missing number in all of the regions.

				2	6
2	3		5	1	
5					6
4					5
	1	3		4	2
	4	2	1		

SAMPLE PUZZLE

1		2	6	4	3
6	4	3	2	5	
5	3		4	1	6
4	2	1	3		5
	6	5	1	3	4
3	1	4		6	2

BINARY PUZZLE

ANSWER PAGE 153

PLACE EITHER A 0 OR 1 INTO EACH EMPTY SQUARE, so that every row and column contains the same quantity of 0s and 1s. There should never be more than two of the same number in a row. For example, 001011 is fine, but 011100 would not be, because there are three ones in a row.

0	0		0		1
		0	1		0
0		0	1		0	1
1		1			0
	1			1		0
1	0		0	1		0
		1	0		
1			1		1	0

SAMPLE PUZZLE

0	0	1	0	1	1
0	0	1	1	0	1
1	1	0	0	1	0
0	1	0	1	0	1
1	0	1	1	0	0
1	1	0	0	1	0

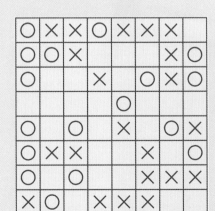

NO FOUR IN A ROW

ANSWER PAGE 153

FILL IN THIS GRID so that every square contains either an O or an X. You must place these so that there are no rows of four (or more) Os or Xs in any direction, including diagonally.

O	X	X	O	X	X	X
O	O	X			X	O
O			X		O	X	O
			O			
O		O		X		O	X
O	X	X			X		O
O		O			X	X	X
X	O		X	X	X	

SAMPLE PUZZLE

O	X	X	X	O	O
X	X	O	O	X	O
X	O	X	X	X	O
X	O	X	O	X	O
O	O	X	O	O	O
O	X	O	X	X	O

MINESWEEPER PUZZLE

ANSWER PAGE 154

MINES ARE HIDDEN IN SOME OF THE EMPTY SQUARES IN THIS GRID. It's your job to figure out where they are and draw a mine in that spot. Luckily, you can figure out exactly where they are by using the number clues.

Each number tells you how many mines there are in the touching squares surrounding each number, which includes diagonally touching squares. Some squares will be left blank.

M	2	2	2	1
2	3	M	M	2
M	2	3	M	2
2	2	2	3	2
M	2	M	2	M

SAMPLE PUZZLE

LETTER BLOCKS

ANSWER PAGE 154

PLACE A LETTER FROM A TO E INTO EACH EMPTY SQUARE, so that no letter repeats in any row, column, or bold-lined region. **Identical letters can't touch—not even diagonally.**

		D		
	E		C	
		A		

SAMPLE PUZZLE

C	A	D	E	B
E	B	C	A	D
A	D	E	B	C
B	C	A	D	E
D	E	B	C	A

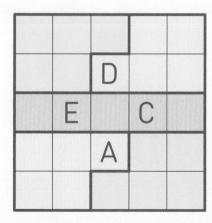

FOUR WINDS PUZZLE

ANSWER PAGE 154

EACH NUMBER TELLS YOU HOW MANY SQUARES YOU MUST CONNECT to it by drawing horizontal and vertical lines from the number. For example, the "4" on the far left of the example has a line above it that travels to 2 squares, and a line below it that travels to 2 squares, for a total of 4. Each line can only connect to a single number. The lines do not cross.

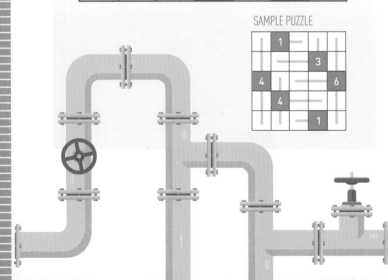

SAMPLE PUZZLE

BRIDGES
ANSWER PAGE 154

DRAW LINES TO CONNECT PAIRS OF CIRCLES. (Their numbers do not need to match.) The number in each circle tells you how many lines connect to that circle. No more than two lines may connect any individual pair. Lines cannot cross one another or cross over another circle.

You must join the circles in such a way that all of the circles are connected. You should be able to start on any circle and follow lines to reach any other circle in the grid.

SAMPLE PUZZLE

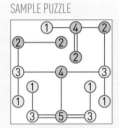

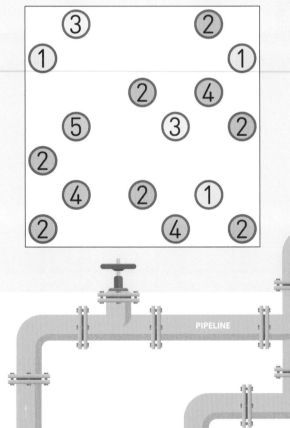

PIPE LINK

ANSWER PAGE 154

Draw a straight line, corner, or cross in each empty square to form a single loop. The loop must travel through every square and then return to where it began.

SAMPLE PUZZLE

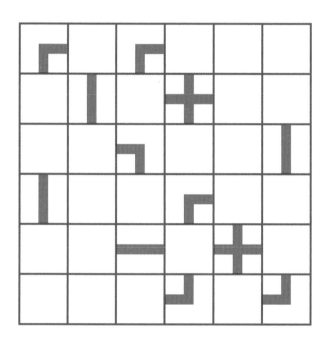

ENTRY AND EXIT

ANSWER PAGE 154

DRAW A LOOP THAT VISITS EVERY SQUARE, using only straight lines and corners. The loop cannot cross itself at any point or enter a square more than once. Once the loop enters a bold-lined region, it must visit every square in that region before it exits that region.

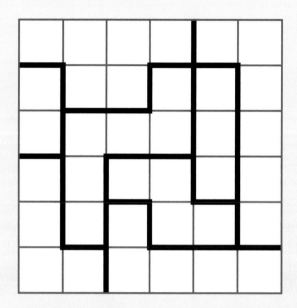

SAMPLE PUZZLE

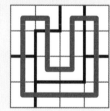

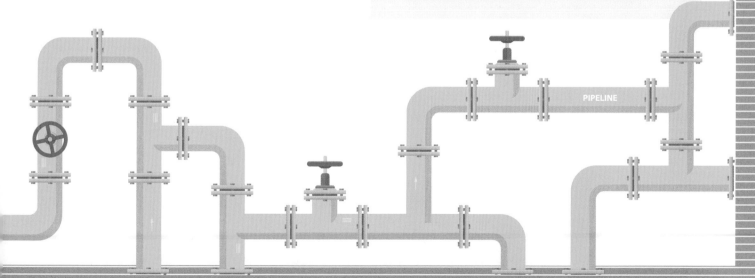

BRICKS ANSWER PAGE 154

PLACE A NUMBER FROM 1 TO 6 into every empty square, so that no number repeats in any row or column. Every bold-lined brick with two squares must contain one even and one odd number.

SAMPLE PUZZLE

6	3	1	2	4	5
2	5	4	6	1	3
1	2	3	4	5	6
3	1	2	5	6	4
5	4	6	1	3	2
4	6	5	3	2	1

	6			3	
	2	1	3	4	
5					1
2					3
	3	6	5	1	
	1			5	

TENS PUZZLE ANSWER PAGE 154

PLACE A NUMBER FROM 0 TO 9 INTO EVERY EMPTY SQUARE, so that no number repeats in any row. Two identical numbers cannot be in touching squares— not even diagonally. Each column of white squares must add up to the number in the green square immediately beneath.

SAMPLE PUZZLE

7	0	8	5	1	4	9	6	2	3
9	4	6	3	2	8	7	1	5	0
1	5	2	9	0	6	4	8	3	7
17	9	16	17	3	18	20	15	10	10

1			2	9	6	7		8	
5	2			4	0				9
	0	8				5	6	3	
7	2	18	12	15	15	20	12	18	16

NUMBER ARROWS

ANSWERS PAGE 154

PLACE A NUMBER from 1 to 4 (first puzzle), 1 to 5 (second puzzle), or 1 to 6 (third puzzle) into every square, so that no number repeats in any row or column. Numbers and arrows outside the grid show you the total sum of all the numbers in the given diagonal.

In the example, the 10 on the top row points at 4, 3, and 3 (as indicated by the orange line), which add up to 10.

HINT: One number on each side of the puzzle points at only a single square, so you can write these numbers in immediately.

SAMPLE PUZZLE

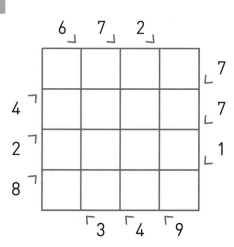

1

2

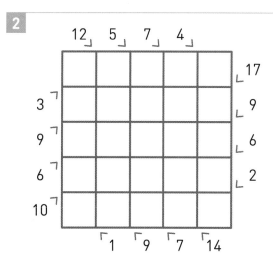

3

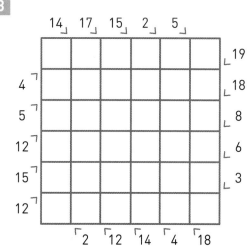

[BEHIND THE BRAIN]

Puzzles like the ones on this page might appear to be "just" math puzzles. The truth is that they require a range of skills beyond simple addition. In particular, you need to use your logical thinking skills. It's how you break down a problem into smaller, easier steps, and it's very important. For example, in the puzzles above, you need to consider each of the number clues around the outside of the grid one by one, until you find a clue that can help you make progress. If you were to simply guess, you'd be unlikely to find the right solution. So every time you come across an unfamiliar problem, pause and first think about the smartest sequence of steps you can take to solve it.

FOLLOWING DIRECTIONS ANSWER PAGE 154

CAN YOU FIND THE HIDDEN TREASURE?

- Start from a square containing a boat, just north of a small island.

- Head west toward shore, and keep going until you are in the middle of a mountain range. If you reach the tropical palms, you have gone too far.

- Turn right and head north, crossing more mountains until you reach a large house.

- Face to your left, and swim across the sea, passing over the place where jellyfish are found.

- When you reach the island, head south until you reach the place where turtles swim. Dive there, and you will find the hidden treasure.

3D ROTATIONS

ANSWER PAGE 155

WHICH ONE OF THESE IMAGES, A TO D, IS A ROTATED VERSION of the same arrangement of cubes shown in blue? Try considering each level of the arrangement separately, rather than looking at the entire arrangement at once.

HINT: You could also try counting the number of cubes on a level; if this differs, you don't need to worry about their exact positions once rotated because you already know they don't match!

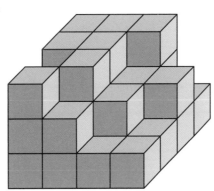

A

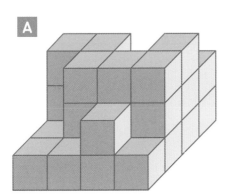

B

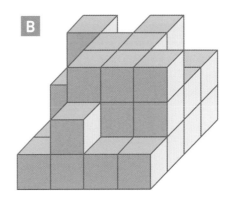

C

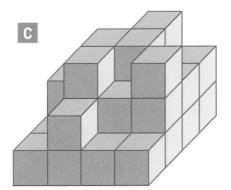

D

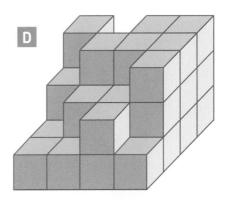

REASSEMBLY REQUIRED

ANSWERS PAGE 155

IMAGINE CUTTING OUT AND REARRANGING THESE FOUR TILES, so that they join together to make a picture. What would that picture show?

1

ANSWER →

like

Now try the same with these four tiles. What would you see if you were to rearrange them and join them together again? It's much trickier this time, since you'll need to imagine rotating the tiles, too!

2

ANSWER →

COMPLETE THE PATTERN

ANSWER PAGE 155

WHICH ONE OF THE TILES, A to D, should replace the green square to complete the pattern?

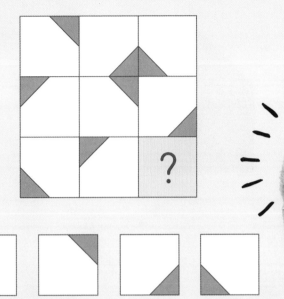

A   B   C   D

COMPLETE THE SEQUENCE

ANSWER PAGE 155

WHICH ONE OF THE TILES, A to D, should come next in this sequence, and why?

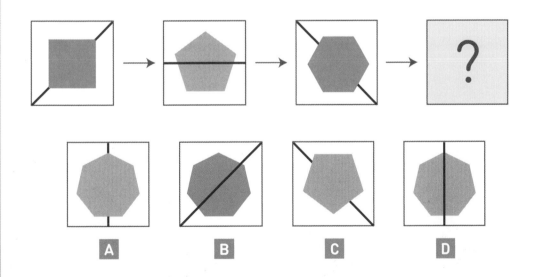

A   B   C   D

COUNTING CUBES

ANSWERS PAGE 155

IMAGINE THAT YOU HAVE various sets of 4 x 4 x 3 block of cubes, arranged like this:

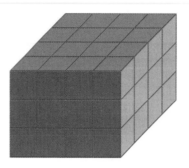

HINT: To make it easier to keep count, you could try counting just the cubes in the top layer, then the middle layer, and then just the bottom layer. Then add together these three totals.

You also have a green and a blue set, which started off looking like the orange set above. However, some cubes have fallen off. How many cubes remain in each of the pictures below? Remember to count the cubes that are hidden underneath other cubes, too.

1

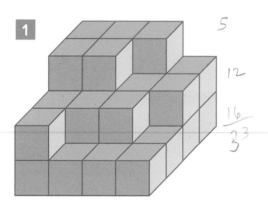

5

12

16

33

2

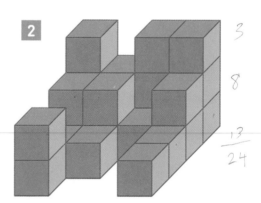

3

8

13

24

[BEHIND THE BRAIN]

How can you look at flat pictures, like the ones above, and easily understand them as 3D pictures? It comes down to the shortcuts your brain takes in order to help you make sense of the world as quickly as possible. Even though you have two eyes that enable you to see how far away things are, your brain doesn't just rely on that information when working out how far away something is. It interprets lots of clues in a scene to speed things along—clues that are present in flat drawings and photographs. It makes a lot of assumptions about straight lines and how they connect to one another—and particularly how angled lines lead away from vertical or horizontal lines. As a result, you don't have any trouble working out how each cube fits into the 3D drawings above.

COMBINING IMAGES ANSWER PAGE 155

IF YOU WERE TO STACK THE FIRST THREE PICTURES on top of one another, without rotating them, which of the tiles below would result? Assume that every picture is transparent.

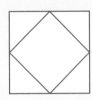

A   B   C   D

COMBINING GRIDS ANSWERS PAGE 155

THE SAME PICTURE IS SHOWN TWICE BELOW. In each case, half of the picture is covered by eight black tiles. Imagine combining the two pictures. Can you answer the following questions?

- How many orange squares are there in total?
- How many blue triangles are there in total?
- How many green circles are there in total?

JIGSAW CUTTING   ANSWER PAGE 155

CAN YOU DRAW ALONG THE GRID LINES TO DIVIDE THIS GRID into four identical shapes? The shapes can be rotated relative to one another, but not reflected. The example shows how it works.

SAMPLE PUZZLE

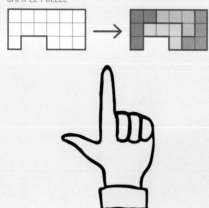

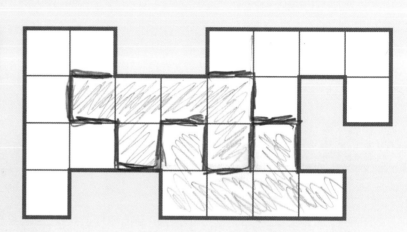

WORD PYRAMID   ANSWER PAGE 155

CAN YOU SOLVE THE CLUES TO FILL THIS PYRAMID? Each row contains the same letters as the row above, plus one extra. You can rearrange the letters on each line, if you need to.

1 | c a t | ← FELINE PET
2 | c h a t | ← TALK CASUALLY
3 | c h e a t | ← GIVE YOURSELF AN UNFAIR ADVANTAGE
4 | d e t a c h | ← SEPARATE SOMETHING FROM SOMETHING ELSE
5 | h a t c h e d | ← CAME OUT OF AN EGG, LIKE A BABY BIRD
6 | t h a t c h e d | ← COVERED IN STRAW, LIKE A VERY OLD HOUSE

SAMURAI SUDOKU ANSWER PAGE 155

This giant puzzle consists of three overlapping 6x6 sudoku grids. Place a number from 1 to 6 into each empty box so that, within each of these three grids, no number repeats in any row, column, or bold-lined 2x3 box. You will need to solve all three grids at the same time in order to arrive at the solution.

SAMPLE PUZZLE

6	2	4	1	3	5						
5	1	2	3	4	6						
3	4	5	6	2	1						
4	3	6	5	1	2	4	3				
1	5	3	2	6	4	5	1				
2	6	1	4	5	3	6	2				
		2	1	4	5	3	6	1	2		
		5	6	3	1	2	4	6	5		
		4	3	2	6	1	5	3	4		
				1	3	4	2	5	6		
				6	4	5	3	2	1		
				5	2	6	1	4	3		

4	5	1	2	6	3		
2	6	4	3	1	5		
3	1	5	6	2	4		
6	4	2	5	3	1	4	6
1	2	3	4	5	6	2	1
5	3	6	1	4	2	3	5

5	2	1	4	6	3	5	2
4	3	6	5	1	2	4	3
1	6	2	3	5	4	1	6
3	1	2	5	6	4
5	2	4	6	3	1
4	6	3	1	2	5

CIRCLE LINK ANSWER PAGE 155

Draw horizontal and vertical lines to join the circles into pairs, so that each pair contains one orange circle and one green circle. Lines can't cross each other, and they also can't cross over another circle. Every circle must be part of exactly **one** pair.

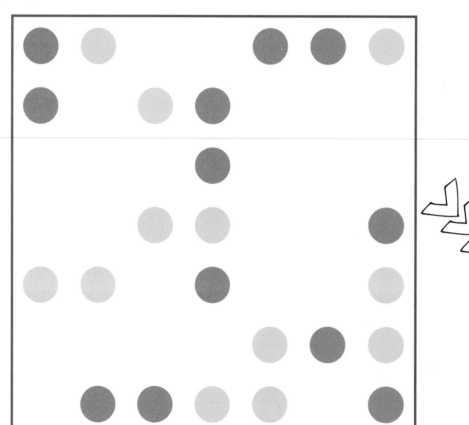

TIME STARTED	TIME ENDED	TOTAL TIME

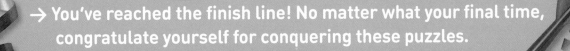

→ You've reached the finish line! No matter what your final time, congratulate yourself for conquering these puzzles.

NUMBER DARTS ANSWER PAGE 155

Add together one number from the outer ring, one from the middle ring, and one from the inner ring so that their sum equals the first total below. Repeat the process so that your sums match the second, then the third total. For example, you could form a total of 14 by adding 3 from the inner ring, 1 from the middle ring, and 10 from the outer ring.

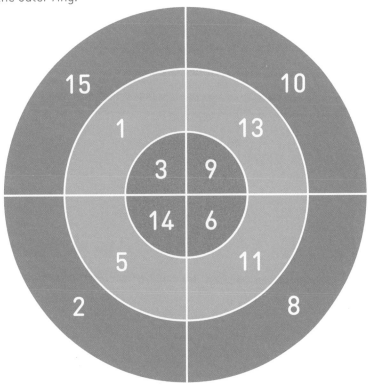

Totals: 15 28 31

TIME STARTED	TIME ENDED	TOTAL TIME
:	:	:

CHAPTER TWO

CIRCLE MAZE PAGE 13

RECTANGULAR MAZE PAGE 16

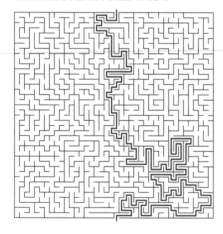

BRIDGE MAZE PAGE 17

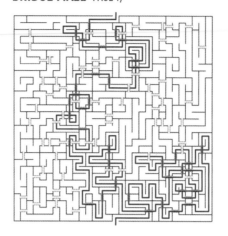

JIGSAW CUTTING PAGE 18

PUZZLE 1

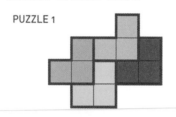

PUZZLE 2

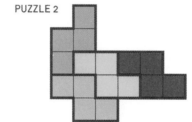

PUZZLE 3

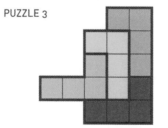

PUZZLE 4

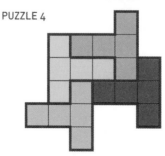

JIGSAW FIT PAGE 19

PUZZLE 1

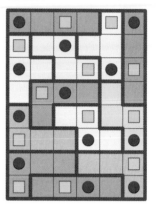

PUZZLE 2

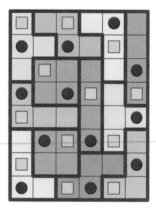

SHAPE LINK PAGE 20

PUZZLE 1

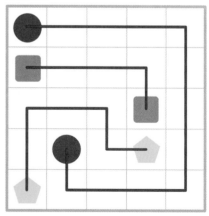

PUZZLE 2

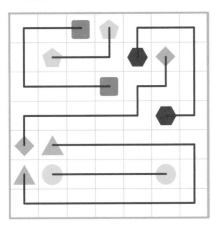

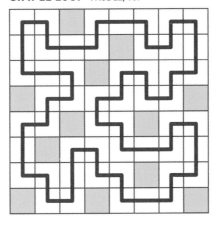

PUZZLE 2

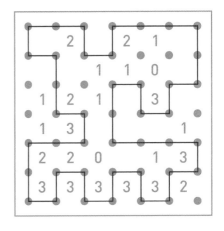

PATHFINDER PAGE 21

PUZZLE 1

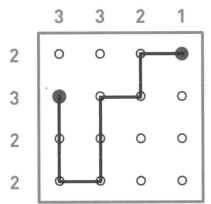

PUZZLE 2

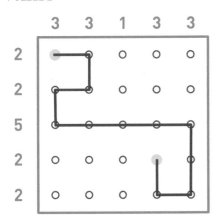

FENCES PAGE 22, BOTTOM

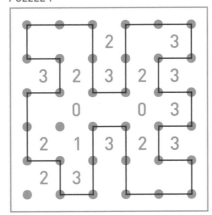

SLITHERLINK PAGE 23

PUZZLE 1

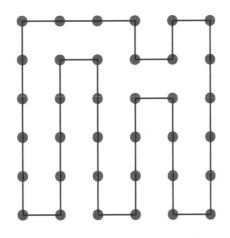

DIVIDED INTO AREAS PAGES 24–25

PUZZLE 1

PUZZLE 2

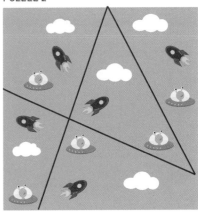

ANSWERS

MEADOWS PAGE 26

PUZZLE 1

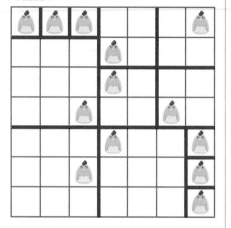

PUZZLE 2

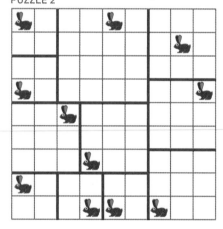

RECTANGLES PAGE 27

PUZZLE 1

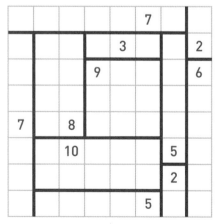

PUZZLE 2

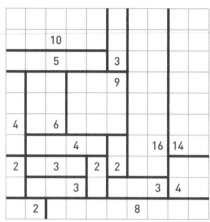

DOMINO ASSEMBLY PAGE 28

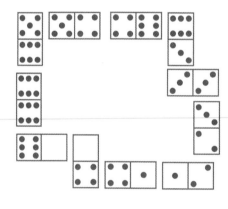

LASERS PAGE 29, TOP

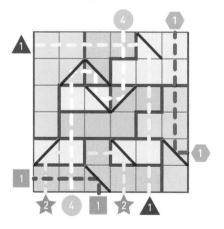

TENTS PAGE 29, BOTTOM

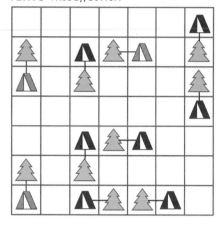

WARP MAZE PAGE 30

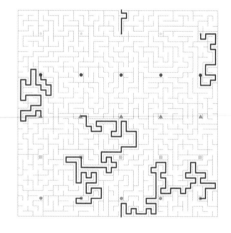

MULTILEVEL MAZE PAGE 31

FLOOR 1

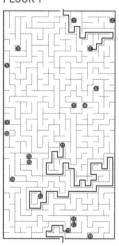

FLOOR 2

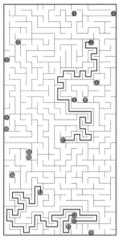

CIRCLE LINK PAGE 32

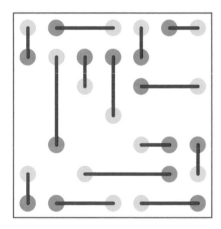

NUMBER DARTS PAGE 33

20 = 2 + 8 + 10
36 = 12 + 14 + 10
39 = 11 + 13 + 15

CHAPTER THREE

MONUMENT MATCHING PAGE 35

1) Statue of Liberty (United States)
2) Taj Mahal (India)
3) Eiffel Tower (France)
4) CN Tower (Canada)
5) Parthenon (Greece)
6) Stonehenge (United Kingdom)
7) Leaning Tower of Pisa (Italy)
8) Sphinx (Egypt)

CHANGING OBJECTS PAGE 38

WORLD CAPITALS PAGE 43

Abu Dhabi – United Arab Emirates
Beijing – China
Berlin – Germany
Brasília – Brazil
Brussels – Belgium
Buenos Aires – Argentina
Cairo – Egypt
Canberra – Australia
London – United Kingdom
Mexico City – Mexico
New Delhi – India
Ottawa – Canada
Paris – France
Rome – Italy
Tokyo – Japan
Washington, D.C. – United States

CONTINENTAL CONFUSION PAGE 44

Argentina – South America
Australia – Australia
Brazil – South America
Canada – North America
China – Asia
Egypt – Africa
Ethiopia – Africa
France – Europe
Germany – Europe
India – Asia
Kenya – Africa
Malaysia – Asia
Mexico – North America
South Africa – Africa
Spain – Europe
United Kingdom – Europe
United States – North America

STATE YOUR LOCATION PAGE 45

A: Montana; B: Maine; C:Texas;
D: Oregon; E: North Carolina;
F: California; G: Arizona; H: Florida;
I: Iowa; J: New York; K: Colorado;
L: Wisconsin

ANIMAL ANTICS PAGE 46

1) Kangaroo – Australia
2) Kiwi – New Zealand
3) Bull – Spain
4) Bald eagle – United States
5) Bear – Russia
6) Carp – Japan
7) Bulldog – Britain
8) Elephant – India
9) Giant panda – China
10) Lion – Kenya

ANSWERS

ILLUSION PATTERNS PAGE 49

Some examples of what you can do include:

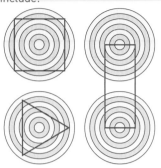

WHO IS NEW? PAGE 50

NAMES AND FACES PAGE 51

Sergio Isabella Nicky William Chris Ava Olivia Liam

CIRCLE LINK PAGE 54

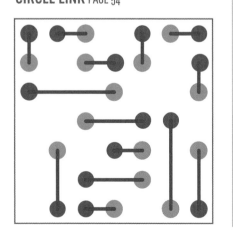

NUMBER DARTS PAGE 55

22 = 2 + 8 + 12
27 = 13 + 8 + 6
37 = 13 + 10 + 14

CHAPTER FOUR

COUNTING CHALLENGE PAGE 57

There are 6 trees.

FRUIT FOR THOUGHT PAGE 60

1)

 = 3

 = 4

 = 2

2)

 = 2

 = 6

 = 1

BALANCED DIET PAGE 61

1)

 Heaviest fruit

Lightest fruit

2)

 Heaviest vegetable

 Lightest vegetable

NUMBER PYRAMID PAGE 62, LEFT

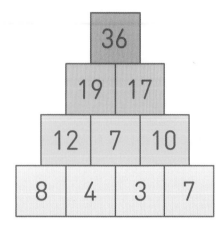

	36		
19	17		
12	7	10	
8	4	3	7

ARITHMETIC SQUARE PAGE 62, RIGHT

1	+	5	+	4	=	10
×		+		×		
3	+	7	+	8	=	18
+		+		+		
2	×	6	+	9	=	21
=		=		=		
5		18		41		

FUTOSHIKI PAGE 63, LEFT

2 > 1	5	4	3
4	5	2	3 > 1
5	2 < 3	1	4
1	3	4 < 5	2
3	4	1	2	5

KAKURO PAGE 63, RIGHT

			\4	\10		
	\3 22	1	2			
\9 16	5	3	1	\17	\16	
\17 9	8	\24 7	7	8	9	
\20 7	9	4	\12 4	5	7	
	\7	2	1	4		
	\4	1	3			

BRAIN CHAINS PAGE 64

19	25	8	9	45	5
5	+7	÷2	×9	-3	+12	63
44	-6	×2	÷4	+11	÷2	15
34	+26	-19	+29	-15	÷11	5

FLOATING NUMBERS PAGE 65
16 = 6 + 10
22 = 4 + 8 + 10
26 = 6 + 9 + 11
32 = 4 + 8 + 9 + 11
40 = 4 + 6 + 9 + 10 + 11

CALCUDOKU PAGE 66

1

6+ 1	2	7+ 3	4
3	5+ 4	6+ 2	1 1
2 2	1	4	6+ 3
7+ 4	3	1	2

2

7+ 4	4+ 1	3	6+ 2
3	6+ 2	3+ 1	4
3+ 1	4	2	4+ 3
2	7+ 3	4	1

CALCUDOKU + - × ÷ PAGE 67

1

4+ 1	8× 2	12× 4	3
3	4	2÷ 1	2
2÷ 2	1	5+ 3	3- 4
7+ 4	3	2	1

2

5+ 3	3+ 2	1	32× 4
2	48× 3	4	1
1	4	2	5+ 3
4	2- 1	3	2

A QUESTION OF AGE PAGE 68, TOP

Isabel is 3; Cecilia is 5; Maria is 8.

SHOPPING PROBLEM PAGE 68, BOTTOM

1) Milk and butter together cost $5.75. Your change will be $4.25.
2) Two milks and one butter cost $8.00. Three cheeses and one juice cost $7.25, making this the cheapest option.
3) Two bills.
The four items total $10.
$10 + $7.50 = $17.50
You need bills that add up to a minimum of $18. To equal exactly $18, you would need four bills: a $10, $5, $2 and $1 bill. Instead, you can use just two bills by giving the cashier two $10 bills.

TIME PUZZLES PAGE 69, LEFT

1) 1:00 p.m.
2) 12:30 p.m.
3) 6:00 p.m.

TIME ZONE PROBLEMS PAGE 69, RIGHT

1) 7 a.m.
2) 9 a.m. tomorrow
3) 5 p.m. tomorrow (in French time, the flight would arrive at 8:30pm)

DICE FACES PAGE 70

1) The dice add to 21
2) The opposite sides add to 13
3A) 3 of the dice could be showing 6
3B) 2 of the dice could be showing 3
3C) The minimum total is 18: (from left to right: 6 + 5 + 2 + 1 + 4)
3D) The maximum total is 28: (from left to right: 6 + 5 + 6 + 5 + 6)

ANSWERS

DOT-TO-DOT DECISIONS PAGE 71

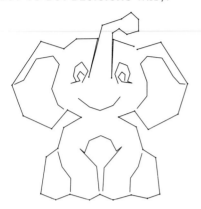

ODD ONE OUT PAGE 72

A) 15, all the rest are even/multiples of two

B) 16, all the rest are multiples of three

C) 50, the sum of the two digits in every other number is 10

D. 56, in every other number, the second digit is lower than the first digit

SEQUENCE SOLVING PAGE 73

A) 8, as shown on the page

B) 7, once deleted, each number is 2 larger than the previous one

C) 24 – once deleted, each number is 3 smaller than the previous one

D) 18 – once deleted, the difference between numbers increases by 1 at each step (that is, the sequence is +1, +2, +3, +4, etc.)

MULTIPLICATION SEARCH PAGE 74

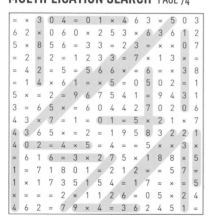

NUMBER TRIANGLES PAGE 75

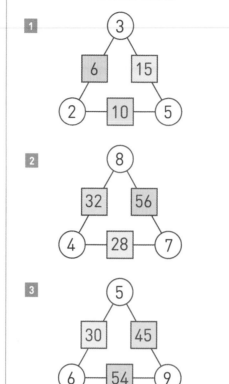

CIRCLE LINKS PAGES 76

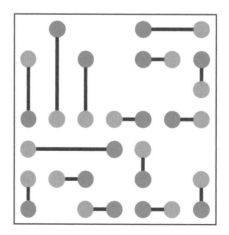

NUMBER DARTS PAGES 76

15 = 3 + 10 + 2

24 = 14 + 8 + 2

32 = 13 + 10 + 9

CHAPTER FIVE

LATERAL THINKING PAGE 90

Lateral thinking puzzles sometimes have more than one possible answer, but here's a possible solution for each of the puzzles:

1) The man is standing on an inside window ledge, and he only fell onto the floor inside the building.

2) When you are eating a watermelon, the red part is good to eat but when you reach the green part (the rind) you should stop. (This also applies when picking fruit—for example, you would normally go ahead and pick red, ripe tomatoes, but stop when you reach a green, unripe tomato).

3) A secret.

LOGICAL THINKING PAGE 91

1) The red toy cost 5¢. This means the blue toy cost $1.05, and so the total price is $1.10.

2) You need to turn over two cards: the letter E (it might not have an even number on the other side) and the number 9 (it might have a vowel on the other side). Most people think that you only need to turn over the E, or think you need to turn over the E and the 4. There's no point in turning over the 4, because it doesn't matter what's on the other side. Whether it's a vowel or not, the rule would not be broken.

3) Yes, a dog is definitely looking at a cat. If Dozy Dave is a cat, then Princess Peach (a dog) is looking at a cat. If Dozy Dave is a dog, then Dozy Dave is looking at Barky Bill (a cat). Either way, a dog is looking at a cat. Many people incorrectly think that you don't have enough information to answer this.

SOME ASSEMBLY REQUIRED PAGE 93

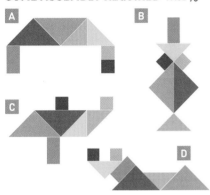

CIRCULAR CHALLENGE PAGE 95

There are many possible 4-color solutions; there is only one 2-color solution, shown here.

CIRCLE LINK PAGE 98

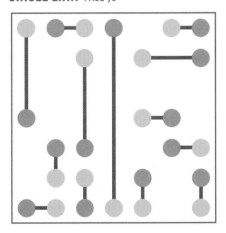

NUMBER DARTS PAGE 99

22 = 14 + 1 + 7
25 = 14 + 1 + 10
28 = 13 + 11 + 4

CHAPTER SIX

WORD ORBIT PAGE 101

The words that can be made include the following:
MAN, MAP, MAR, MEN, RAN, RAP, REP, RIP, SAP, SIN, SIP, SIR, TAN, TAP, TAR, TEN, TIN, and TIP.

OPPOSITES PAGE 104, TOP

STOP–GO; WHITE–BLACK; SLOW–FAST; SOFT–HARD; BRAVE–COWARDLY; FUTURE–PAST; FORGET–REMEMBER; START–FINISH; NIGHT–DAY; DARK–LIGHT; SAFE–DANGEROUS; GUILTY–INNOCENT; EASY – DIFFICULT; FIRST–LAST

PREFIXES AND SUFFIXES PAGE 104, BOTTOM

Prefixes:
AUTOBIOGRAPHY, EXTRAORDINARY, INTERNATIONAL, OVERCOOK, SEMICIRCLE
Suffixes:
AFFORDABLE, FORGIVENESS, KINGDOM, LEADERSHIP, THOUGHTLESS

SETS PAGE 105

COLORS
Blue
Brown
Lavender
Yellow

FRUIT
Cherry
Lemon
Orange
Pineapple

METALS
Bronze
Gold
Silver
Tin

PRECIOUS STONES
Diamond
Emerald
Ruby
Sapphire

ANAGRAMS PAGE 106

COLORS
1) RED
2) BLUE
3) PINK
4) GREEN
5) WHITE
6) PURPLE

FRUITS
1) PLUM
2) BANANA
3) BLUEBERRY
4) KIWI
5) NECTARINE
6) WATERMELON

ANAGRAM SENTENCES PAGE 107

1) She squirted LEMON juice onto the MELON to keep it fresh.
2) He saw the CAT jump up, then ACT very strangely.
3) His leg ACHES, every time they CHASE the dog.
4) When he stopped to LISTEN, he noticed that it was completely SILENT.
5) He went into his STUDY, and noticed how DUSTY his desk was.
6) The UNWARY bird wandered onto the RUNWAY.
7) The SKATER left STREAKS on the ice.
8) When she was STRESSED, she sometimes ate too many DESSERTS.

WORD LADDERS PAGE 108, TOP

BEE
BEG
BIG
PIG

COW
COP
POP
PUP
PUG

WORD PYRAMID PAGE 108, BOTTOM

ONE; NOTE; STONE; HONEST; SHORTEN

WORD STACKS PAGE 109, TOP

Puzzle 1
ADD: BADDEST, ADDRESS, PADDLING, SADDLE
Puzzle 2
RED: CREDITS, INGREDIENT, PREDICT, TIREDNESS

LINK WORDS PAGE 109, BOTTOM

1) FOOT, to make BAREFOOT and FOOTBALL
2) LIGHT, to make DAYLIGHT and LIGHTHOUSE
3) STAR, to make SUPERSTAR and STARFISH

ANSWERS

PHRASE FINDER PAGE 110

T	H	E		B	E	S	T		W	A	Y
	T	O		P	R	E	D	I	C	T	
Y	O	U	R		F	U	T	U	R	E	
I	S		T	O		C	R	E	A	T	E
	I	T									

INTERPRETATION REQUIRED
PAGE 111, LEFT
1) A piece of cake
2) Read between the lines
3) Missed the boat
4) Make a long story short
5) Raining cats and dogs
6) Better late than never

PICTURE PHRASES PAGE 111, RIGHT
1) The last straw (or the final straw)
2) Once in a blue moon

WORD FIT PAGE 112

P	A	R	E	N	T	S		L	O	V	E
A		U		I		S		U		U	
C	A	R	A	V	A	N		A	F	T	E	R
T		A		I		S		R		R	O
R	U	L	E	R		E	A	R	W	I	G
E		E		O		L		A		C	T
S	P	R	I	N	G		A	N	C	H	O	R
S		E		M		S		G		O	
	A	D	V	E	N	T		E	X	C	E	L
E		U		N		A		M		A	L
Y	A	C	H	T		T	R	E	M	B	L	E
E		E				U		N		L	Y
S	I	D	E		W	E	A	T	H	E	R

WORD PATH SEARCH PAGE 113, LEFT

A	N	A	I	R	I	I	N
R	C	P	N	B	T	A	A
F	E	S	A	R	T	S	U
O	C	I	L	H	I	N	A
M	E	X	I	C	Y	N	I
L	A	G	A	R	M	A	N
R	T	U	G	E	A	C	D
O	P	A	D	A	N	A	I

WORD GRID SEARCH PAGE 113, RIGHT

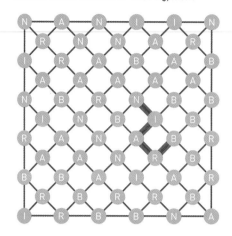

SINGLE-WORD WORD SEARCH
PAGE 114, TOP

M	E	G	E	G	M	G	A	S	A
E	S	E	S	A	A	S	E	M	E
M	E	G	A	E	S	S	M	S	A
E	E	E	A	S	G	M	E	M	A
M	M	E	E	S	E	M	E	M	S
G	S	E	S	M	A	M	E	S	M
S	G	A	M	E	M	M	A	E	G
G	A	E	S	E	M	M	G	G	G
S	S	G	E	G	A	G	A	S	M
S	A	M	M	A	S	S	A	G	S

WRAPAROUND WORD SEARCH
PAGE 114, BOTTOM

U	O	P	K	S	O	Y	U	N	O
N	R	U	W	M	O	S	E	C	C
U	N	O	O	C	H	P	C	N	C
K	H	W	M	I	A	O	O	H	A
P	L	S	S	P	M	O	C	N	R
U	C	R	O	P	S	E	N	I	P
N	U	T	O	N	T	P	O	O	C
M	M	O	U	S	E	M	O	A	R
A	O	U	O	O	R	U	A	E	N
S	N	S	S	S	H	O	T	R	O

MISSING MIDDLE WORD SEARCH
PAGE 115

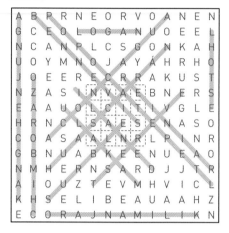

A	B	P	R	N	E	O	R	V	O	A	N	E	N
G	C	E	O	L	O	G	A	N	U	O	E	E	L
N	C	A	N	P	L	C	S	G	O	N	K	A	H
U	O	Y	M	N	O	J	A	Y	Á	H	R	H	O
J	O	E	E	R	E	C	R	R	A	K	U	S	T
N	Z	A	S	I	N	V	A	E	B	N	E	R	S
E	A	A	U	O	L	C	I	T	I	V	G	L	E
H	R	N	C	L	S	A	E	S	E	N	A	S	O
C	O	A	S	A	A	L	N	R	L	P	I	N	R
G	B	N	U	A	B	K	E	E	N	U	E	A	O
N	M	H	E	R	N	S	A	R	D	J	J	T	R
A	I	O	U	Z	T	E	V	M	H	V	I	C	L
K	H	S	E	L	I	B	E	A	U	A	A	H	Z
E	C	O	R	A	J	N	A	M	I	L	I	K	N

WORDS WITHIN WORDS PAGE 116, TOP
1) Black: The ca<u>b lacked</u> doors.
2) Brown: My eye<u>brow nearly</u> got removed.
3) Yellow: She used to <u>yell, ow</u>ing to her bad knee.
4) Green: The o<u>gre en</u>dangered them all.
5) Purple: The railway <u>spur pleased</u> the town.
6) Orange: You can go to the bakery <u>for angel</u>ic, delicious desserts!
7) White: The co<u>w hit</u> every fence as it tried to escape.
8) Scarlet: Thi<u>s car let</u> her drive more easily.

MINI CODEBREAKER PAGE 116, BOTTOM
LION; DOLPHIN; LEOPARD; SNAKE.
Mystery animal: KOALA.

INITIAL SEQUENCES PAGE 117, TOP
1) Numbers in increasing value: one, two, three, four, five, six, seven
2) Planets, moving outward from the sun: Mercury, Venus, Earth, Mars, Jupiter, Saturn, Uranus
3) Colors of the rainbow in order: red, orange, yellow, green, blue, indigo, violet
4) Number positions (which are known as "ordinal numbers") in increasing order: first, second, third, fourth, fifth, sixth, seventh

CODEBREAKER PAGE 117, BOTTOM
Congratulations on revealing the secret text.

WORD CIRCLE PAGE 118, LEFT
The word that uses every letter is "fingers." Other words to be found include feign, feigns, fen, fens, fern, ferns, fin, fine, finer, fines, finger, fins, fringe, fringes, gin, gins, grin, grins, infer, infers, ins, reign, reigns, rein, reins, resign, resin, ring, rings, rinse, risen, sign, signer, sin, sine, sing, singe, singer, and siren.

WORD SQUARE PAGE 118, RIGHT
The word that uses every letter is "butterfly." Other words to be found include blur, blurt, burly, but, butler, butt, butte, butter, elf, flu, flutter, fly, fret, fur, furl, let, lure, rely, rub, rule, rut, truly, tub, turf, turtle, utter, and utterly.

WORD SLIDER PAGE 119
Words to be found include dared, darer, dares, direr, dived, diver, dives, dorms, dosed, doses, doves, fares, farms, faves, fired, firer, fires, firms, fiver, fives, fores, forms, laser, lived, liver, lives, livid, lores, loris (a slow-moving nocturnal Asian monkey-like animal), loser, loses, loved, lover, and loves.

CIRCLE LINK PAGE 120

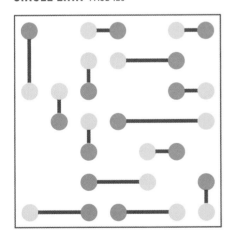

NUMBER DARTS PAGE 121
18 = 1 + 15 + 2
23 = 6 + 15 + 2
32 = 12 + 15 + 5

CHAPTER SEVEN

STRAW PUZZLE PAGE 123

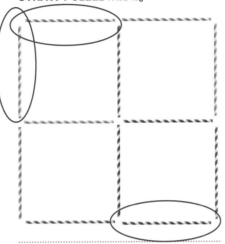

TOUCHY PAGE 126, TOP

1	3	2	6	4	5
6	4	5	1	3	2
3	2	6	4	5	1
4	5	1	3	2	6
2	6	4	5	1	3
5	1	3	2	6	4

TRIO SUDOKU PAGE 126, BOTTOM

1	5	2	6	4	3
3	4	6	5	2	1
5	1	4	3	6	2
2	6	3	4	1	5
4	2	5	1	3	6
6	3	1	2	5	4

JIGSAW SUDOKU PAGE 127, TOP

1	5	6	4	2	3
4	6	2	3	1	5
6	4	1	5	3	2
3	2	5	1	6	4
5	1	3	2	4	6
2	3	4	6	5	1

BLACKOUT SUDOKU PAGE 127, BOTTOM

1	5	■	2	6	4
2	3	4	5	1	■
5	■	1	4	2	6
4	2	6	3	■	5
6	1	3	■	4	2
■	4	2	1	5	3

BINARY PUZZLE PAGE 128, TOP

1	0	0	1	0	0	1	1
0	1	0	1	0	1	1	0
0	0	1	0	1	1	0	1
1	0	1	0	1	0	0	1
0	1	0	1	0	1	1	0
1	0	1	0	1	0	0	1
0	1	1	0	1	0	1	0
1	1	0	1	0	1	0	0

NO FOUR IN A ROW PAGE 128, BOTTOM

O	X	X	O	X	X	O
O	O	X	O	X	O	X
O	O	X	X	O	X	O
X	X	O	O	O	X	X
O	O	X	O	X	O	X
O	X	X	O	X	X	O
X	O	O	X	O	O	X
X	O	O	X	X	O	O

ANSWERS

MINESWEEPER PUZZLE PAGE 129, TOP

🔴		2	2	1
2	3	🔴	🔴	2
🔴		3	🔴	2
2			3	
🔴	2	🔴	2	🔴

LETTER BLOCKS PAGE 129, BOTTOM

D	A	E	B	C
B	C	D	A	E
A	E	B	C	D
C	D	A	E	B
E	B	C	D	A

FOUR WINDS PUZZLE PAGE 130, LEFT

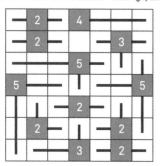

BRIDGES PAGE 130, RIGHT

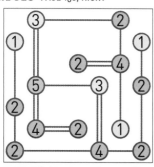

PIPE LINK PAGE 131, LEFT

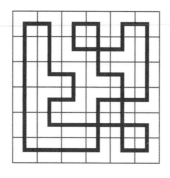

ENTRY AND EXIT PAGE 131, RIGHT

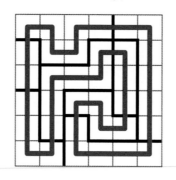

BRICKS PAGE 132, TOP

1	6	5	2	3	4
6	2	1	3	4	5
5	4	3	6	2	1
2	5	4	1	6	3
4	3	6	5	1	2
3	1	2	4	5	6

TENS PUZZLE PAGE 132, BOTTOM

1	0	4	2	9	6	7	5	8	3
5	2	6	3	4	0	8	1	7	9
1	0	8	7	2	9	5	6	3	4
7	2	18	12	15	15	20	12	18	16

NUMBER ARROWS PAGE 133

1

	6	7	2	
	4	1	3	2	7
4	1	3	2	4	7
2	2	4	1	3	1
8	3	2	4	1	
		3	4	9	

2

	12	5	7	4	
	3	5	1	2	4	17
3	4	3	2	1	5	9
9	2	1	5	4	3	6
6	5	2	4	3	1	
10	1	4	3	5	2	
	1	9	7	14		

3

	14	17	15	2	5	
	4	2	6	3	1	5	19
4	3	5	4	2	6	1	18
5	1	3	2	4	5	6	8
12	5	1	3	6	2	4	6
15	6	4	1	5	3	2	3
12	2	6	5	1	4	3	
	2	12	14	4	18		

FOLLOWING DIRECTIONS PAGE 134

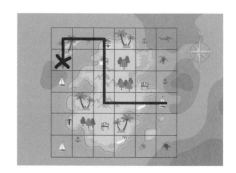

3D ROTATIONS PAGE 135

D

REASSEMBLY REQUIRED PAGE 136

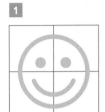 

COMPLETE THE PATTERN PAGE 137, TOP

Tile B. Reading left to right, and then top to bottom, the tile rotates 90 degrees clockwise at every step.

COMPLETE THE SEQUENCE PAGE 137, BOTTOM

Tile D. The number of sides on the shape increases at each step, plus the red line rotates by 45 degrees. The red line also moves in front of and then behind of the shape, and the color of the shape alternates between green and blue.

COUNTING CUBES PAGE 138

1) There are 33 green cubes: 5 on the top layer, 12 on the middle layer, and 16 on the bottom layer.
2) There are 24 blue cubes: 3 on the top layer, 8 on the middle layer, and 13 on the bottom layer.

COMBINING IMAGES PAGE 139, TOP

C

COMBINING GRIDS PAGE 139, BOTTOM

There are 5 orange squares
There are 7 blue triangles
There are 5 green circles

JIGSAW CUTTING PAGE 140, TOP

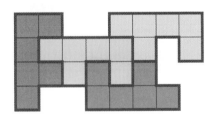

WORD PYRAMID PAGE 140, BOTTOM

1) CAT
2) CHAT
3) CHEAT
4) DETACH
5) HATCHED
6) THATCHED

SAMURI SUDOKU PAGE 141

4	5	1	2	6	3			
2	6	4	3	1	5			
3	1	5	6	2	4			
6	4	2	5	3	1	4	6	
1	2	3	4	5	6	2	1	
5	3	6	1	4	2	3	5	
		5	2	1	4	6	3	5	2
		4	3	6	5	1	2	4	3
		1	6	2	3	5	4	1	6
				3	1	2	5	6	4
				5	2	4	6	3	1
				4	6	3	1	2	5

CIRCLE LINK PAGE 142

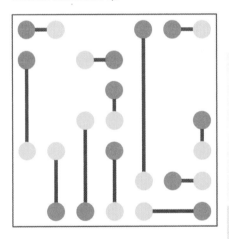

NUMBER DARTS PAGE 143

15 = 6 + 1 + 8
28 = 9 + 11 + 8
31 = 3 + 13 + 15

INDEX

Boldface indicates illustrations.

INDEX

PHOTO CREDITS

ALL PUZZLES: DR. GARETH MOORE. ALL ILLUSTRATIONS, UNLESS NOTED BELOW: MODUZA DESIGN.

AS: ADOBE STOCK; ASP: ALAMY STOCK PHOTO; GI: GETTY IMAGES; SS: SHUTTERSTOCK

COVER (BACKGROUND), NISHIHAMA/SS; (MAZE), GRANDEDUC/SS; (UP RT), OBER-ART/SS; (DOODLES), PAKET/SS; (LO RT), MIKHAIL MISHCHENKO/GI; (LO LE), WAVE-BREAKMEDIA/SS; (UP LE), SHCHERBAKOV ILYA/SS; (UP CTR), PHOTKA/SS; SPINE, PAKET/SS; BACK COVER (BACKGROUND), NISHIHAMA/SS; (CTR), BIORAVEN/SS; (LO LE), PHOTOMASTER/SS; **FRONT MATTER:** 2-3 (BACKGROUND), NISHIHAMA/SS; 2 (DOODLES THROUGHOUT), PAKET/SS; 2 (LO), RANDY RIMLAND/SS; 3 (MAZE), GRANDEDUC/SS; 3 (UP), VALDISSKUDRE/AS; 4-5 (HEXAGON BACKGROUND THROUGHOUT), YANIE/SS; 4 (UP), PHOTKA/SS; 4 (LO), ROMAN SIGAEV/SS; 5 (UP), PIUS LEE/DREAMSTIME; 5 (LO), WAVEBREAKMEDIA/SS; **CHAPTER ONE:** 6-7 (MAZE BACKGROUND THROUGHOUT), GRANDEDUC/SS; 6 (STICKIES THROUGHOUT), MARTINA V/SS7 (CTR RT), ADVENT/SS; 7 (LO), CHRIS_B_PARIS/AS; 8 (HATS), TIERNEY/AS; 8 (BRAIN), ERAXION/GI; 8 (LO), SCIENCE SOURCE; 8 (CONFETTI), PIXELLIEBE/SS; 9 (UP LE), THE PRINT COLLECTOR/ASP; 9 (UP RT), SCIENCE HISTORY IMAGES/ASP; 9 (CTR RT), HISTORICAL IMAGES ARCHIVE/ASP; 10 (LE), HISTORY AND ART COLLECTION/ASP; 10 (RT), ADVENT/SS; 11 (UP LE), MISSTUNI/GI; 11 (UP RT), RIDO/AS; 11 (LO), CHAIKOM/SS; **CHAPTER TWO:** 12 (LO), CALLISTA IMAGES/ASP; 13 (EMOJI THROUGHOUT), OBER-ART/SS; 14 (LO), ADVENT/SS; 15 (UP), NOBEASTSOFIERCE SCIENCE/ASP; 15 (CTR), WDCN/UNIV. COLLEGE LONDON/SCIENCE SOURCE; 15 (LO), IMAGE SOURCE/GI; 16-17 (BACKGROUND), NAYPONG/AS; 18 (UP), COOLAM/SS; 18 (LO), NITIKORNFOTOLIA/AS; 19 (LO), NERTHUZ/AS; 20, ANDRII MUZYKA/AS; 21 (UP), NEW AFRICA/AS; 21 (LO), PARNTAWAN1987/AS; 22-23 (BACKGROUND), BITS AND SPLITS/AS; 22, PHOTOSMATIC/SS; 23, ERIC ISSELÉE/AS; 24-25 (BACKGROUND), TOMERTU/SS; 24 (UP), ESVETLEISHAYA/SS; 24 (ANIMALS), TOPVECTORS/AS; 24 (LO), SONSEDSKAYA/SS; 24 (HELMET), GLENDA POWERS/AS; 25 (UP), ERIC ISSELÉE/AS; 25 (HELMET), GLENDA POWERS/AS; 25 (CHICK), ALEKSS/AS; 25 (LO), VOYAGER624/SS; 26-27 (BACKGROUND), DIM DIMICH/SS; 26 (UP), NYNKE/AS; 26 (ANIMALS), TOPVECTORS/AS; 27 (UP), PETS IN FRAMES/SS; 27 (LO), ARLEE/AS; 28-29 (BACKGROUND), PHOTOPEN/AS; 28 (UP), VIPERAGP/AS; 29 (LO), MAKSYM PROTSENKO/AS; 30, GUNAYALIYEVA/AS; 31, 2265524729/SS; 32-33 (TRIANGLE BACKGROUND THROUGHOUT), MELAMORY/SS; 33 (UP), SUPACHAI SUMRUBSUK/SS; 33 (CHICK), ALEKSS/AS; **CHAPTER THREE:** 35 (1), STEVE COLLENDER/SS; 35 (2), BYELIKOVA OKSANA/SS; 35 (3), DENNIS DOLKENS/DREAMSTIME; 35 (4), LISA CHARBONNEAU/SS; 35 (5), PHOTODISC; 35 (6), CEDRIC WEBER/SS; 35 (8), PIUS LEE/DREAMSTIME; 35 (7), FEDOR SELIVANOV/SS; 36, MERANNA/SS; 37 (UP LE), ZINKEVYCH/SS; 37 (UP RT), RA2 STUDIO/AS; 37 (CTR), JPEGPHOTOGRAPHER/SS; 37 (LO RT), JOHANNES GERHARDUS SWANEPOEL/DREAMSTIME; 37 (LO LE), VITSTUDIO/SS; 38 (BOATS), JULES_KITANO/AS; 38 (BEAR), OVYDYBORETS/DREAMSTIME; 38 (WOODEN SPOON), BERND SCHMIDT/SS; 38 (PAN), ANTON STARIKOV/SS; 38 (PAIL), PHOTODISC; 38 (PLATE), WITTHAYAP/SS; 38 (HEADPHONES), IGOR LATECI/SS; 38 (FORK), PHOTODISC; 38 (ROCKET), 3D_MAN/SS; 38 (OLD CAR), JASMINKAM/SS; 38 (NEW CAR), ANDREY LOBACHEV/SS; 38 (PEN), J. BACKGROUND/SS; 38 (SILVER SPOON), IGOR KOVALCHUK/SS; 39 (PENCIL), YURY SHIROKOV/DREAMSTIME; 40 (UP), ALEXLMX/SS; 41 (UP), ADRIAN LUBBERS; 41 (FRAME), PEERAWIT/SS; 41 (LO), OPENRANGESTOCK/SS; 42-43 (BACKGROUND), ANNA M.N./AS; 43 (UP), MICHAEL KRAUS/SS; 43 (LO RT), SAMANTHAINALAOHLSEN/SS; 43 (LO LE), HOLUBLU6/AS; 45 (LE), ERIC ISSELÉE/AS; 45 (UP), TOMMYBRISON/SS; 46 (UP), SONSEDSKAYA/AS; 46 (BULL), ALBERTO /AS; 46 (BEAR), ROSA JAY/SS; 46 (CARP), ERIC ISSELÉE/AS; 46 (LION, PANDA, EAGLE, KIWI), ERIC ISSELÉE/SS; 46 (DOG), WILLEECOLE PHOTOGRAPHY/SS; 46 (ELEPHANT), VLADIMIR WRANGEL/AS; 46 (KANGAROO), ISSELÉE/DREAMSTIME; 47, FER GREGORY/SS; 48, JAMES STEIDL/AS; 49, RIMMAORPHEY/SS; 50 (ALL), RAWPIXEL.COM/AS; 51 (TOP ROW: A, G, H), RAWPIXEL.COM/AS; 51 (TOP ROW: B, C, D, E, F), MARKUS MAINKA/AS; 52-53 (BACKGROUND), MAGDAL3NA/AS; 52, BILLIONPHOTOS.COM/AS; 53 (UP), TARZHANOVA/AS; 53 (LO), SASHKIN/SS; 55, SUPACHAI SUMRUBSUK/SS; **CHAPTER FOUR:** 57 (TREES), BEGUIMA/AS; 58, ROMARIO IEN/AS; 59 (UP LE), SERGEY NIVENS/AS; 59 (UP RT), ROB/AS; 59 (CTR), SNVVSNVVSNVV/SS; 60 (UP LE), ALEXA_SPACE/AS; 60 (APPLE), DENPHUMI/AS; 60 (BANANA), MAKS NARODENKO/SS; 60 (ORANGE), NEW AFRICA/AS; 60 (PINEAPPLE), INGRAM; 60 (BERRY), MAKS NARODENKO/SS; 60 (APRICOT), VOLFF/AS; 61 (UP), BAIBAZ/AS; 61 (GRAPES), ANASTYA/AS; 61 (PINEAPPLE), ANASTYA/AS; 61 (ORANGE), ANASTYA/AS; 61 (PUMPKIN), LA GORDA/SS; 61 (CABBAGE), LA GORDA/AS; 61 (EGGPLANT), LA GORDA/AS; 61 (POTATO), BOYKO.PICTURES/AS; 62-63 (BACKGROUND), HUAFENG207/SS; 62, ANDRIANO/SS; 63, LOVELY PET/SS; 64-65 (BACKGROUND), KONSTANTIN L/SS; 65 (BALLOONS), GRIVINA/AS; 65 (LO), SAMUEL B./AS; 66, MARJANNEKE DE JONG/SS; 67 (UP), MAYBEIII/AS; 67 (LO), TALVI/SS; 68 (UP), TOBKATRINA/SS; 68 (CTR), HUE TA/SS; 69 (UP), JEFF LUEDERS/SS; 69 (LO), ROMAN SIGAEV/SS; 70, DENIS FONCHIKOV/AS; 71 (UP), DORAZETT/AS; 71 (LO), DORAZETT/AS; 72-73 (CTR), VALDISSKUDRE/AS; 73 (UP), NADI/AS; 73 (LO), CHONES/AS; 74-75 (LO), RMID/AS; 75, BESTV/SS; 77 (UP), SUPACHAI SUMRUBSUK/SS; **CHAPTER FIVE:** 79, SORAYUT/AS; 80 (MUG), VIACHESLAV KRISANOV/DREAMSTIME; 80 (UP RT), MADLEN/SS; 80 (LO RT), HURRICANEHANK/SS; 80 (LO LE), ALEKSWOLFF/AS; 81 (UP LE), DAISY DAISY/AS; 81 (UP RT), HURRICANEHANK/SS; 81 (CTR RT), OLGA KHOROSHUNOVA/AS; 81 (LO), KLETR/SS; 82, VECTORTWINS/AS; 82 (LO LE), ABLUECUP/AS; 83 (TOOLS), STOCK_VEC-TORSALE/SS; 83 (LO LE), FLASHON STUDIO/AS; 84 (MONSTERS), SSTOCKER/AS; 84 (MARKERS), LUNATICTM/AS; 84 (BOXES), PICSFIVE/AS; 85 (MONSTERS), OSOV/SS; 86, LEOBA/GI; 87 (UP), JAVIER BROSC/SS; 87 (LO RT), VALE_ZMEYKOV/SS; 88 (CTR LE), KHUNASPIX/DREAMSTIME; 88 (CTR RT), ISSELEE/DREAMSTIME; 88 (LO RT), GSAGI/GI; 89, CHROMATIKA/AS; 90 (UP), AFRICA STUDIO/AS; 90 (LO LE), GEORGIA EVANS/SS; 91 (UP), INOMASA/SS; 91 (LO), LILUN_LI/GI; 92 (UP), ERIC ISSELÉE/AS; 92 (LO), YELLOW CAT/SS; 93, MISUNSEO/AS; 94-95 (ALL), PETER HERMES FURIAN/AS; 94 (LE), CAT BOX/SS; 95 (RT), GLOBALP/GI; 96-97 (PAPERS), PRANTHIRA/SS; 96, KOZAK SERGII/SS; 99 (UP), SUPACHAI SUMRUBSUK/SS; **CHAPTER SIX:** 100, KUES1/AS; 102, METAMORWORKS/AS; 103 (UP LE), JCFOTOGRAFO/AS; 103 (UP RT), RAW-PIXEL.COM/AS; 103 (CTR RT), MASHE/AS; 104, SAMUEL B./AS; 105 (UP), TIM UR/AS; 105 (LO RT), ANDRIUS GRUZDAITIS/AS; 105 (LO LE), SCIENCE PHOTO/AS; 106 (UP), GLOBALP/GI; 106 (LO), SIMONE/AS; 107, FOTOPARUS/AS; 108, NEJURAS/AS; 109 (UP), STUDIOVIN/SS; 109 (LO), 9DREAMSTUDIO/AS; 110-111 (DIMES), MATTES IMAGES /AS; 110 (UP RT), WAVEBREAKMEDIAMICRO/AS; 111 (STRAWS), NPAVELN/AS; 111 (LO), NASA GODDARD; 112 (LE), AARON AMAT/AS; 113 (PINATA), PHOTOMELON/AS; 113 (FLAG), DEREK BRUMBY/AS; 113 (LO RT), ESBEN468635/AS; 114 (UP), IGOR KOVALCHUK/AS; 114 (LO), ULTRASHOCK/SS; 115, KRIS DEMESA/SS; 116 (UP), AMI MATARAJ/SS; 116 (CTR), CHONES/SS; 116 (LO), NEIRFY/AS; 117, TUPUNGATO/SS; 118-119 (BACKGROUND), LAURA PASHKEVICH/AS; 118, RUSLAN GILMANSHIN/AS; 119, BIG BLUE/AS; 120 (UP), SUPACHAI SUMRUBSUK/SS; **CHAPTER SEVEN:** 123 (CTR), NPAVELN/AS; 123 (LO RT), TASHKA2000/AS; 124 (LE), ANDREY POPOV/AS; 124 (RT), COURTESY RMIT UNIVERSITY; 125 (UP LE), FATCAMERA/GI; 125 (UP RT), ELENA ELISSEEVA/SS; 125 (CTR RT), SANJA KARIN MUSIC/AS; 125 (GAME), VORTEX/SS; 125 (LO RT), JUNCE11/AS; 126 (CTR), FOOD TRAVEL STOCKFORLIFE/SS; 127 (UP), DUDAREV MIKHAIL/AS; 127 (LO), OLIVER HOFFMANN/SS; 128-129 (BACKGROUND), OLLY/AS; 128, BURITORA/AS; 129, GLENDA POWERS/AS; 130, YOD77/AS; 131, KMIRAGAYA/AS; 132-133 (BACKGROUND), DMITRY_EVS/AS; 132 (UP), JIANG ZHONGYAN/SS; 132 (LO), JENSON/SS; 134 (MAP), LEMBERGVECTOR/AS; 134 (LO RT), LAST19/AS; 135, GRANTOTUFO/DREAMSTIME; 136, PRESSMASTER/AS; 137, SAILINGAWAY/AS; 138, KAESLER MEDIA/SS; 139, MARCO ULIANA/AS; 140, SONSEDSKAYA/AS; 141 (UP), CHANAWAT/AS; 141 (LO), MARK BRANDON/SS; 143 (UP), ZAMUROVIC/AS; 143 (DART), SUPACHAI SUMRUBSUK/SS; **END MATTER:** 160 (LO), NYNKE/AS

CREDITS

For all the masterminds. —S.W.D.

For my little boy, Theo, who brings so much joy into our lives. —G.M.

Since 1888, the National Geographic Society has funded more than 12,000 research, exploration, and preservation projects around the world. The Society receives funds from National Geographic Partners, LLC, funded in part by your purchase. A portion of the proceeds from this book supports this vital work. To learn more, visit natgeo.com/info.

For more information, visit nationalgeographic.com, call 1-877-873-6846, or write to the following address:

National Geographic Partners
1145 17th Street N.W.
Washington, DC 20036-4688 U.S.A.

Visit us online at nationalgeographic.com/books

For librarians and teachers: nationalgeographic.com/books/librarians-and-educators

More for kids from National Geographic: natgeokids.com

National Geographic Kids magazine inspires children to explore their world with fun yet educational articles on animals, science, nature, and more. Using fresh storytelling and amazing photography, *Nat Geo Kids* shows kids ages 6 to 14 the fascinating truth about the world—and why they should care.
kids.nationalgeographic.com/subscribe

For rights or permissions inquiries, please contact National Geographic Books Subsidiary Rights: bookrights@natgeo.com

Designed by Rachael Hamm Plett, Moduza Design

Trade paperback ISBN: 978-1-4263-3675-1

The publisher would like to acknowledge the following people for making this book possible: Stephanie Warren Drimmer, narrative text author; Dr. Gareth Moore, puzzle creator and puzzle text author; Kathryn Williams and Kristin Baird Rattini, project editors; Sanjida Rashid, art director; Sarah J. Mock, senior photo editor; Anne LeongSon and Gus Tello, design production assistants.

Printed in China
20/RRDS/1